Praise for *The Wallet Allocation Rule*

Praise from Business Leaders

This is it! Finally, something definitive about what it takes to win the battle for share of customers' hearts, minds, and wallets. Backed by rock-solid science, *The Wallet Allocation Rule* is a definite must-read.

> —Peter Jueptner, executive vice president of Strategy and New Business Development, Esteé Lauder Inc.

The authors expose Net Promoter as *The Emperor's New Clothes* and explain a superior metric that brings in the dimension of competition, providing managers with an effective way to drive beyond traditional customer satisfaction to achieve goals for profitability, market share, and growth. Groundbreaking work for marketing leaders and a must-read. *The Wallet Allocation Rule* is the next big thing!

> —Jim Welch, director, PwC's PRTM Management Consulting

Living in the world of big data analytics, we strive to turn customer satisfaction into customer retention using measured techniques every single day. *The Wallet Allocation Rule* delivers a concrete approach to trace our value to our enterprise clients, giving us structure to increasing market capture. This is groundbreaking indeed.

> —Rama S. Moorthy, CEO, Hatha Systems

The Wallet Allocation Rule is brilliant. Managers need to change their thinking on the importance of rank and how they can position their brand to meet their financial goals. The simplicity of the mathematical model underscores the common sense of the Wallet Allocation Rule. I have a feeling this concept will be applied effectively by enlightened organizations. I enjoyed reading this book and kept thinking that this has a *Freakonomics*-like quality to it.

> —Tom D'Orazio, CEO, Superna Life Sciences

The Wallet Allocation Rule is groundbreaking research with clear, practical applications. It is well written and thought provoking. I'll never look at general marketing assumptions the same again. A must-read!

> —Kevin P. Kaseff, president, Titan Real Estate Investment Group, Inc.

Satisfaction from your customers means nothing if it doesn't increase your share of wallet! *The Wallet Allocation Rule* gives you the hard facts and fills the void in how to do exactly that. Not just stories but real strategies to grow your business, your brand, and wow your customers. Just read it!

—Chester Elton, *New York Times* best-selling author of *All In* and
What Motivates Me

I like this book. The authors bring data and analyses to demolish widely held but misplaced beliefs in the efficacy of the Net Promoter Score, customer satisfaction, customer loyalty, and other popular measures in causing improvements in growth, market share, and profitability. They put the Wallet Allocation Rule to the test, and it performs. The book is an easy and fast read, with great case studies and charts. The appendices should be helpful to those wishing to put the rule to the test in their own companies.

—George Stalk, senior advisor, The Boston Consulting Group

The Wallet Allocation Rule is that rare, valuable combination of being strategically insightful and empirically powerful. This creates a path forward for better, data-driven decisions on how to capture more share of wallet while not getting caught in any of the classic pitfalls of satisfying customers without seeing impact.

—James Mendelsohn, chief marketing officer, CAN Capital

Assumption, so the saying goes, is the mother of all f**k-ups. And yet, as demonstrated in *The Wallet Allocation Rule,* marketers have been happily throwing money at customer experience management despite the absence of hard evidence of a correlation between customer satisfaction and share of wallet. Over the course of this thought-provoking book, authors Keiningham, Aksoy, Williams, and Buoye convincingly pick apart the suitability of existing satisfaction and reputational metrics at predicting customer spend and posit a potential solution to the problem—the Wallet Allocation Rule. Explaining the scientific foundation for the rule and its practical applications, readers finally have the missing link within their grasp—the ability to link their existing customer metrics to share of wallet.

—Neil Davey, editor, MyCustomer.com

I've been following Timothy Keiningham's research and thought-provoking books for over a decade due to our mutual interest in customer loyalty. His most recent book, *The Wallet Allocation Rule,* is simply brilliant. After years of arguing about which metric is best, this groundbreaking book reveals what really matters: how your brand compares to your competitors' in your customer's mind.

—Bob Thompson, CEO, CustomerThink and author of *Hooked On Customers:*
The Five Habits of Legendary Customer-Centric Companies

The Wallet Allocation Rule addresses one of the largest challenges I see running Loyalty360. We are privileged to speak to CMOs [chief marketing officers] on a daily basis, and the biggest challenge they face is keeping up with the disparate technology challenges they are confounded with today. The clarion call is metrics; brands are confounded with the best internal metrics, as well as competitive benchmarking metrics by which to gauge the efficacy of their efforts; *The Wallet Allocation Rule* is one of the best books I have seen that addresses the metrics and insights needed to gauge said efficacy. Having known Tim for many years, the passion he has for brands to enable them to create truly (behaviorally based) loyal customers (advocates) has never wavered, and this book is the zenith of this passion.

—Mark Johnson, CEO and CMO of Loyalty360

Companies need to focus on customer metrics that drive business results. *The Wallet Allocation Rule* does a nice job of putting people's attitudes in context of their real-world choices, which, in turn, provides a more direct connection with actual customer behavior.

—Bruce Temkin, managing partner of Temkin Group, cofounder and chair of the Customer Experience Professionals Association (CXPA)

To achieve better business results, it's essential to rise above the myths and common practices, to adopt superior insights and methods. This book walks you through the fallacies in current thinking and shows empirical evidence that explains incorrect assumptions and proves correct interpretations. Readers will discover revolutionary insights and techniques that can propel them out of their customer experience ROI [return on investment] plateau to achieving strong growth.

—Lynn Hunsaker, founder and head of ClearAction Customer Experience Optimization

Praise from Academic Leaders

The Wallet Allocation Rule convincingly dispels well-established myths about customer satisfaction and provides a new metric for predicting market share growth across competing brands. The authors demonstrate through examples, data, and cases that customer satisfaction and NPS [Net Promoter Score] alone are not enough. These *must* be measured relative to competitors, and the Wallet Allocation Rule is the way to do this. If your goal is market share leadership, this book is a must-read!

—Mary Jo Bitner, professor and Edward M. Carson Chair, Arizona State University, Editor, *Journal of Service Research*

The Wallet Allocation Rule is an unabashed challenge to the current state of marketing within organizations. It eviscerates the navel-gazing customer satisfaction focus of most organizations seeking growth through customer experience management. But the book isn't just a critique of current practice. It provides a real, scientifically vetted solution to the problem—something sorely lacking for the highly touted but soon discounted management buzzwords. This book is certain to be one of the most important business books of the decade.

—Edward C. Malthouse, Theodore R. and Annie Laurie Sills Professor of Integrated Marketing Communications, Northwestern University

In today's metrics-driven age, a new metric that companies will benefit from knowing is how high up they are in their customers' shopping budgets. The historically popular metrics of satisfaction and purchase intent have been shown to have little or no predictive power in gauging actual purchases/repurchases. These metrics also do not offer managers information on what proportion of money consumers are willing to spend on their brand and whether their competitors are being chosen over them. After all, a pat on the wallet is a better proof of the pudding than a pat on the back. *The Wallet Allocation Rule* presents revolutionary insights that redefine the measurement of customer loyalty. With the help of this book, managers can not only gain a new perspective on the wallet share their brands command but also learn tools they can implement to maximize this share and cement their spot in their customer's shopping lists.

—V. Kumar, Regents Professor and Richard and Susan Lenny Distinguished Chair, Georgia State University

The Wallet Allocation Rule cogently debunks commonly held beliefs about the merits of conventional CSAT metrics and offers a simple—yet powerful—alternative for capturing and capitalizing on how customers actually allocate their spending among competing brands. Succinctly written and filled with easy-to-grasp illustrations, this thought-provoking book is a must-read for anyone interested in understanding the determinants of market share and revenue growth.

—A. Parasuraman, James W. McLamore Chair of Marketing, University of Miami

This book challenges the strongly held belief that customer satisfaction and its various derivatives, such as Net Promoter Score, are leading indicators of firm performance. Using rigorous research, the authors show that there is a weak correlation between satisfaction (and its variants) and consumers' purchase behavior. What matters is satisfaction relative to competition, not absolute satisfaction scores that almost all companies rely on. The authors translate this idea into a simple but powerful Wallet Allocation Rule. This book will change the way you think about customer satisfaction.

—Sunil Gupta, Edward W. Carter Professor of Business Administration, Harvard Business School

Keiningham and colleagues lay bare the "managerially correct" fallacy that by merely improving customer satisfaction and Net Promoter Score levels, firms will automatically see market share growth and higher customer spending. This well-researched book blasts these myths. More important, it shows managers precisely what to do (and how to do it!) to improve their firm's share. Grounded in strong research, *The Wallet Allocation Rule* is destined to have a lasting impact on both the science and practice of management.

—Katherine N. Lemon, Accenture Professor of Marketing, Carroll School of Management, Boston College

The Wallet Allocation Rule is a thought-provoking book that will change the way leading enterprises will measure and manage customer satisfaction. And I love that this book is based on solid academic research that will pass the test of time.

—Jochen Wirtz, professor of Marketing, National University of Singapore

The Wallet Allocation Rule focuses on a very important strategic issue for all business executives—how to win the battle for share of wallet. Backed by numerous examples and solid research, this book provides a new lens for viewing marketing decisions. The authors convincingly show that a focus on satisfaction is a recipe for financial disaster. Using the Wallet Allocation Rule, managers can finally make the critical link to share of wallet.

—Bo Edvardsson, professor and founder of CTF-Service Research Center and Vice Rector Karlstad

If you cannot measure it, you cannot manage it. In this book Keiningham, Aksoy, and Williams let managers become *real* managers by employing KPIs [key performance indicators] that measure what really matters: investments that drive share of wallet. I wish I wrote this book. I am delighted I read it!

—Tor W. Andreassen, professor of Marketing and director of the Center for Service Innovation at NHH Norwegian School Economics

This book is essential reading for anyone who wants to know how to improve customers' buying behavior. The *Wallet Allocation Rule* is an insightful strategy for those business executives who have the task of guiding their companies toward a new understanding of their customers' spending patterns. I am sure this book will be on every executive's desk.

—Jay Kandampully, professor in Services Management and Hospitality, The Ohio State University, Editor, *Journal of Service Management*

Customer satisfaction is hugely important, but its relationship to share of wallet depends in large part on the competition. Superstar consultant Tim Keiningham and his colleagues at Ipsos Loyalty have teamed with academic Lerzan Aksoy to help unlock exactly how it is that satisfaction relates to share of wallet. Based in large part on actual corporate applications, *The Wallet Allocation Rule* is a readable book that should be valuable to all managers who want satisfying their customers to pay off.

—Roland T. Rust, Distinguished University Professor and David Bruce Smith Chair in Marketing, University of Maryland

This is a fantastic book that will help organizations better manage, monitor, and understand their customers from the perspective of better managing their profits. It advances the conversation from customer satisfaction and Net Promoter Score to share of wallet thereby paving the way to linking behavioral metrics to financial metrics. The intellectual advances in the book will be relevant for both academics and practitioners, not just today but for decades to come.

—Vikas Mittal, J. Hugh Liedtke Professor of Marketing, Jones Graduate School of Business, Rice University

THE
WALLET
ALLOCATION
RULE

THE
WALLET
ALLOCATION
RULE

Winning the Battle for Share

Timothy Keiningham • Lerzan Aksoy • Luke Williams

with Alexander Buoye

WILEY

Customers have a logical reason for using every brand that they do. Therefore, the secret to success lies in giving customers fewer reasons to use the competition.

Contents

much as they like your brand. The end result is that you are losing sales. To understand what drives share of wallet and ultimately market share, managers need to shift their focus from the drivers of satisfaction or NPS to the drivers of rank. Our research conclusively proves that the rank that customers assign to a brand relative to other brands they use predicts share of wallet using a simple, previously unknown formula, which we've named the Wallet Allocation Rule.

Chapter 3

The Wallet Allocation Rule in Action 51

Key Takeaway: The drivers of share of wallet are almost always very different from the drivers of satisfaction or NPS. Wallet Allocation Rule analysis gets to the heart of what drives wallet share by identifying what drives customers' preference for your brand vis-à-vis competition instead of simply determining what makes customers happy.

Chapter 4

Customers as Assets 89

Key Takeaway: Growth is easy for firms willing to give their products away—for as long as they remain in business! But the first duty of a business is to survive. Managers must never lose sight of the fact that the end goal is profits, not just revenues.

Chapter 5

New Metrics That Matter for Growth 109

Key Takeaway: The Wallet Allocation Rule makes it possible for managers to easily link customer satisfaction to share of wallet. But because the rule is based upon a company's relative rank, not its absolute satisfaction level, firms need to add new metrics to their list of Key Performance Indicators (KPIs).

Chapter 6

Making It Happen 129

Key Takeaway: Rather than end this book with a cheerleader's call to "Go, Fight, Win!" we instead want to focus on this all too important fact: Without proper execution, good ideas can and often do fail. The Wallet Allocation Rule is no exception. We end by identifying the most common failure points, and what you can do to avoid them.

Afterword

What's Next? 139

Preface

It's never enough to tell people about some new insight ... Instead of pouring knowledge into people's heads, you need to help them grind a new set of eyeglasses so they can see the world in a new way. That involves challenging the implicit assumptions that have shaped the way people have historically looked at things.[1]

—John Seely Brown, cochairman of the Deloitte Center for the Edge and past chief scientist for Xerox Corporation

The impetus for this book began as a quest for an answer to a problem that quite literally had shaken us to our core. We have dedicated our careers to helping companies win through improved customer loyalty. Throughout our careers, however, we consistently found that most of the things we were told about loyalty were wrong.

With each new set of myths we uncovered, we sought to set the record straight. We coauthored several books (*Loyalty Myths,*[2] *Return on Quality,*[3] *The Customer Delight Principle,*[4] and *Why Loyalty Matters*[5]) and award-winning papers so that the business community could gain from our insight and avoid the pitfalls we found.

But there was one overwhelming problem that we could not explain away: The measures we use to gauge customers' perceptions of their experience (e.g., satisfaction and Net Promoter Score) are so weakly correlated to customers' share of category spending with the brands that they use that the metrics are managerially irrelevant.

This problem challenged everything we believed about customer satisfaction and loyalty. Specifically, we expect more satisfied and loyal customers to devote more of their spending to a brand. That expectation is the primary reason that efforts to improve satisfaction and loyalty are supposed to be good business decisions.

The truth was horribly bad. On average, customers' satisfaction (or Net Promoter Score) levels explain around 1 percent of the variation in customers' share of category spending. No good manager knowingly makes decisions about how to allocate a company's scarce resources based on a 1 percent model fit.

The reality, however, is that we have in effect been doing this every time we ask managers to focus on improving the customer experience to improve business outcomes. Sadly, the purportedly better-fitting models presented to managers to justify these efforts are almost always based on very bad statistics.

The result has been that businesses seldom see meaningful returns on their efforts to improve the customer experience. Not surprisingly, this has caused managers to question using these metrics to guide their businesses.

Given the seriousness of the problem, we were compelled to see if there was a better way. We began an intensive investigation to uncover why satisfaction and other commonly used metrics do not link to customers' share of spending.

The result of this investigation was the discovery of the Wallet Allocation Rule, a simple formula that managers could use to determine the share of wallet that customers allocated to their brands.

The Wallet Allocation Rule was introduced in the *Harvard Business Review*[6] and received the Next Gen Disruptive Innovation Award.[7] It has been subjected to rigorous scientific investigations.[8] In addition, many of the strategies and tactics outlined in this book were introduced in the *MIT Sloan Management Review*.

Our goal in writing this book is to make businesses' efforts to improve customer satisfaction and loyalty pay dividends by giving them a tool that we have proved works. We believe strongly that companies that apply the Wallet Allocation Rule can distinguish themselves in the eyes of both their customers and their shareholders.

Foreword

Is there a strong link between your company's customer satisfaction or Net Promoter Score levels and the share of spending that customers allocate to your brand? We suspect that if we polled managers from virtually any firm, the consensus would be "Yes!"

Unfortunately, almost none of them would have the evidence to actually support this belief. Traditional metrics designed to gauge customers' perceptions of the brands that they use do a terrible job of correlating with customers' share of wallet levels. This is a serious problem.

For most firms, the greatest financial opportunity from improving satisfaction and loyalty is getting customers to allocate a greater percentage of their spending to a brand—far more than the impact of improved retention rates or referrals. Without the ability to link satisfaction to customers' share of spending, it is almost impossible for managers to determine what to do to improve customers' buying behaviors. Consequently, the return on efforts to improve the customer experience is frequently trivial, even negative.

Despite an abundance of books, articles, and speeches on the importance of the customer experience to business success (and a host of metrics that purport to guide managers to this success), to date there has been no easy-to-use system for managers to gauge performance that meaningfully links to customers' spending behaviors. As a result, "proof" of success has too often been limited to anecdotal evidence that seldom proves applicable to other companies.

This book fills that void. It provides a new and rigorously tested approach—the Wallet Allocation Rule—that is proved to link customer satisfaction and other commonly used metrics to share of wallet.

The Wallet Allocation Rule is at once a profound, award-winning *Harvard Business Review*–published thought leadership and a return to the fundamentals of business success from which managers stray at their peril. The practical principles detailed in this book provide managers with the tools they need to win where it counts most—in their customers' spending.

Henri Wallard
Deputy CEO, Ipsos
Chairman of Ipsos Loyalty, Ipsos MediaCT, and Ipsos Public Affairs

Ralf Ganzenmueller
CEO, Ipsos Loyalty

It's "Oh My God!" Bad

Marketing is too important to be left to the marketing department.[1]

—*David Packard, cofounder and past chairman, chief executive officer (CEO) and president of Hewlett-Packard*

- "Marketing measures ROI [return on investment] in terms of marketing, such as customer satisfaction and brand value instead of the most relevant relationship, the one between spending and the gross profit generated from these investments … brand value! What in God's name is this anyway? It's not as if our shareholders care." (CEO of a Spanish telecommunications firm)
- "There is a disconnect between our overall strategy and what marketing understands to be our customers." (CEO of an Austrian retailer)
- "Marketers are, simply put, often disconnected from the financial realities of the business." (CEO of a German financial institution)
- "Marketers make decisions based upon gut feelings rather than a solid ROI analysis." (CEO of a U.S. professional services firm)[2]

CEOs around the world have stopped trusting their chief marketing officers (CMOs). Our research proves it.[3] The findings are sobering.

The majority of CEOs can't bring themselves to say that marketing is strategically relevant.[4] Oh my God!

This is a major problem. Marketing's job is to bring the voice of the customer to the company. Customers are the only reason companies exist, and marketing is charged with overseeing the customer experience. In fact, 90 percent of CMOs are *personally* responsible for the overall customer experience management efforts of their firms.[5]

Unfortunately, for many corporate leaders marketing has become, to quote the CEO of an Italian telecom, a "function not on the top of my everyday priority list."[6] Or worse! CEOs often view marketing as a money pit. To quote the CEO of one U.S. retailer, "Marketing [has] great ideas but no clue how to measure its impact on what really counts. . . . How can I allocate them a budget that disappears into a black box while others can deliver me an ROI for every dollar I give them?"[7]

Marketing's detractors likely don't see a problem at all—and to be sure, there are lots of detractors. Ironically, for a management science charged with managing the reputation of their companies, marketing has a terrible reputation among consumers and business professionals.[8] Only 10 percent of the population has a positive impression of marketing. By contrast, 62 percent have a negative opinion of marketing. Moreover, detractors can rightfully point out that companies still exist and that companies must, by definition, have customers. So companies can exist just fine without much help from marketing. What difference does it make that *marketing* has lost strategic relevance with CEOs?

The reason is best summed up in the words of Peter Drucker, the father of modern management.

> There is only one valid definition of business purpose: To create a customer. . . . Because it is its purpose to create a customer, any business enterprise has two—and only these two—basic functions: marketing and innovation. They are the entrepreneurial functions. Marketing is the distinguishing, the unique function of the business. Any organization in which marketing is either absent or incidental is not a business and should never be run as if it were one.[9]

Marketing's failure will ultimately be reflected in the customer experience. In fact, it already is. Given the current CEO-CMO breakdown, it's not surprising to find a corresponding breakdown between the way senior executives view their companies and the way their customers do. After all, it's marketing's job to be the champion of the customer for the CEO. What is surprising, however, is the enormity of the gap. A study reported in the *Harvard Management Update* finds that 80 percent of company executives believe that their companies provide a "superior" customer experience. Only 8 percent of their customers agree.[10] This finding is confirmed in the Temkin Group report, "The State of Customer Experience Management, 2014," which found that only 10 percent of firms are customer centric.[11]

Of course, positive change for customers will happen only when CEOs view their companies from their customers' perspective. After all, there's no need to change things when you believe you are already doing a superior job.

It is easy to blame CEOs for being shortsighted. The sad truth is that CEOs' complaints about marketing are valid. Marketers do a terrible job of linking their efforts to tangible business outcomes. To be fair to CMOs, it isn't for lack of desire or effort. The problem is more pernicious. All too often, the expected linkage isn't there—and it never was! The underlying assumptions CMOs use to justify most of their investments in improving the customer experience are wrong.

Growth Is Hard to Find

CEOs at every public company are obsessed with achieving two outcomes: profits and growth. The reason for profits is obvious: Profits determine a company's viability.

It is growth, however, that is the lifeblood of companies. It is arguably the most important gauge of a company's long-term success. It is what creates economic value for shareholders. As a result, growth is the common goal of every CEO of a public company and one of the most important metrics by which the board of directors will assess a CEO's performance.

Unfortunately, growth is a goal that is seldom achieved. An investigation of 4,793 public companies reported in the *Harvard Business Review* found that fewer than 5 percent achieved net income growth of at least 5 percent every year for five years.[12] Furthermore, once growth stalls, the odds of ever resurrecting even marginal growth rates are very low.[13] Consequently, although there is no question that growth is the imperative, the dismal results for most companies prove that it's hard to know just how to make it happen.

Deconstructing Market Share

If the goal is market share growth, then we need to begin by understanding what actually drives market share. Strangely, although growth is the goal of virtually every CEO of every public company, few managers know the main components of market share. Virtually all managers calculate market share as follows:

$$Market\ share = \frac{sales\ revenue}{total\ market\ revenue}$$

In other words, they simply take the sales figure for their firm or brand and divide this by total sales for the category.

The good news is that this is technically correct. The bad news is that it provides no strategic guidance for growing market share. To do that, managers need to understand the impact of three distinct components that drive the market shares of all firms:[14]

1. *Penetration:* This is the proportion of customers within an industry category who use your brand at least once in a given time period.[15] It is calculated as follows:

$$Penetration\ share = \frac{customers\ who\ have\ purchased\ the\ brand\ (\#)}{customers\ who\ have\ purchased\ a\ product\ in\ the\ category\ (\#)}$$

2. *Usage:* This is a measure of how heavily customers of your brand use products in the category relative to all customers in that same category.[16] It is calculated as follows:

$$Heavy\ usage\ index = \frac{average\ total\ purchases\ in\ category\ by\ brand\ customers\ (\#,\ \$)}{average\ total\ purchases\ in\ category\ by\ all\ customers\ in\ category\ (\#,\ \$)}$$

3. *Share of wallet:* This is the percentage of your customers' spending in the category that is allocated to your brand.[17] It is calculated as follows:

$$Share\ of\ wallet = \frac{brand\ purchases\ (\#,\ \$)}{\substack{total\ category\ purchases \\ by\ brand\ buyers\ (\#,\ \$)}}$$

Looked at this way, the formula for market share becomes as follows:

$$Market\ share = penetration\ share \times heavy\ usage\ index$$
$$\times share\ of\ wallet$$

Viewing market share as a function of these different components points us toward three very different strategies for growth.

A *penetration* strategy is all about acquiring new customers. This means persuading potential customers to try the brand and expanding into new markets. Without question, acquiring new customers will always be vital to the success of any business. As markets become saturated, however, it gets more and more difficult to find new potential customers. In fact, lower demand and higher competition in the developed world has caused some of the most-respected brands to chase growth in the developing world.

A *usage* strategy is about getting consumers of your brand to increase their total consumption in the category. In other words, if your brand can get its customers to buy more in the category than competitors do, your market share will increase. It's a good idea if you can do it. For example, we are aware of one toilet bowl cleaner that wanted to increase usage of its product to increase its market share. Unfortunately, convincing consumers to clean their toilets more frequently wasn't a realistic option. Instead, the company increased the size of the opening on the spout used to spray the cleaner into the toilet. The result was that more cleaner went down the toilet, and hence the bottles ran out sooner, thereby requiring more frequent purchases of the product.

For most categories, however, getting customers to buy more is very difficult to do. Need tends to drive most of our purchases. For example, we don't tend to buy more toothpaste when we start making more money (and we probably wouldn't even if they increase the size of the opening on the tube).

A *share of wallet* strategy is about getting your customers to allocate a greater percentage of their spending in the category to your brand. It is almost always easier and more cost-effective to improve current customers' share of spending with a firm (i.e., share of wallet) than it is to acquire new customers. This is because, in most categories today, consumers are not loyal to *a* firm or *a* brand but rather by a *set* of firms and brands.

This means that more customers alter their spending patterns instead of completely halting business with a firm. Therefore, efforts designed to manage customers' spending patterns tend to represent far greater opportunities than simply trying to maximize customer retention rates. For example, a study by Deloitte finds that nearly 50 percent, on average, of hotel loyalty members' annual hotel spend is not with their preferred brand.[18] Moreover, a study by McKinsey finds that the cost of lost wallet share typically exceeds the cost of customer defections. For example, McKinsey found that on average 5 percent of bank customers close their checking accounts each year; the impact of losing these customers results in a loss of 3 percent of the banks total deposits. By contrast, 35 percent of customers reduced their share of deposits each year, resulting in a loss of 24 percent of total bank deposits.[19] Moreover, they observed this same effect for all 16 of the industries that they examined.

Although managers need to consider how each component of market share fits into their firms' overall growth strategies, share of wallet is the factor most directly affected by the customer experience. After all, share of wallet is arguably the most important gauge of a customer's loyalty—in fact, in their seminal *Harvard Business Review* paper, business consultant Thomas Jones and esteemed Harvard professor W. Earl Sasser, Jr., assert that share of wallet is "the ultimate measure of loyalty."[20] Clearly, loyalty builds as the result of consistently positive customer experiences.

As a result, both CEOs and CMOs make customer loyalty a top priority. Seventy percent of CMOs rank customer loyalty as a top three strategic priority for their firms—93 percent put it in their top five.[21] Similarly, CEOs consistently rank customer relationships in their top challenges—in fact, a recent global survey of CEOs found that this challenge is second only to getting top caliber employees.[22]

To achieve this goal, firms worldwide have adopted holistic customer experience management programs with the clear aim of improving the share of business that customers allocate to their brands. In fact, 65 percent of companies have a senior executive in charge of their company's customer experience efforts.[23] And to help these companies, an entire industry has developed to maximize the customer experience at all points of contact within a company.[24] The result is that companies spend billions of dollars each year to improve the customer experience.

To ensure that these efforts are positively affecting customer loyalty, most CMOs measure and manage customers' satisfaction and recommend intention levels (see Figure 1.1). In fact, marketing executives frequently rank customer satisfaction as their number one priority.[25] Why? Because managers believe that spending on the customer experience results in the following chain of effects: customer experience → customer satisfaction → share of wallet.

Unfortunately, it doesn't work out that way. Although the goal is admirable and the focus on the customer experience is imperative, managers are unable to connect their efforts to improve the customer loyalty metrics that they track with business growth. Spending more money on the customer experience often doesn't result in happier customers.[27] Probably more critical for managers, improved satisfaction rarely leads to improved market share.

To find out why, we undertook an intensive investigation into the relationship between satisfaction and business outcomes. Our

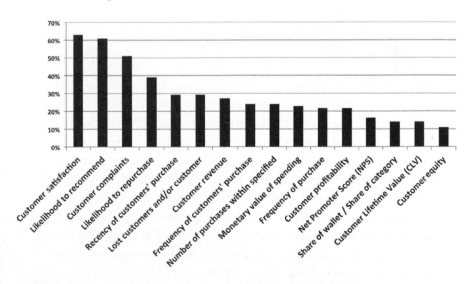

FIGURE 1.1 Customer Loyalty Metrics Tracked by CMOs[26]

research—conducted with Professor Sunil Gupta at the Harvard Business School—uncovered two critical issues that have a strong negative impact on translating customer satisfaction into positive business outcomes. Moreover, these issues are equally applicable for other commonly used metrics, such as recommend intention and the Net Promoter Score (NPS).[28] These two problems can be summarized as follows:

1. Satisfaction ≠ market share
2. Satisfaction ≠ share of wallet

Given the serious potential for damaging the financial performance of a company, these findings should affect every company's customer experience strategy.

Different Metric, Same Outcome

Before discussing the two most common problems, it is important for managers to understand that whether your firm tracks satisfaction, recommend intention, NPS, or some other commonly used customer survey–derived metric, you are unlikely to get managerially relevant differences in terms of their relationship to growth. This is because these metrics are actually measuring the same underlying construct—specifically, how positively customers feel toward the brand.[29] So the argument that one metric works significantly better in linking to growth is not only erroneous but has been conclusively proved to be false in all large-scale peer-reviewed scientific investigations.[30]

Our own research clearly and easily demonstrated the fallacy of the "my metric is best" argument. We examined the NPS, which was sold as "the single most reliable indicator of a company's ability to grow."[31] To see whether that was indeed the case, we chose to examine the same data used to make this claim. Specifically, we replicated the charts used in the book *The Ultimate Question* by Fred Reichheld, the creator of NPS. These charts were used to demonstrate the performance of NPS in linking to growth. Because these industries were specifically selected for presentation in the book, they would clearly be expected to serve as the best examples of the relationship between NPS and growth.[32]

Without question, the strength of the relationship between NPS and business growth presented in these charts was impressive. But was it superior to other metrics? To find out, we used the data from these charts to compare NPS levels with customer satisfaction, specifically the American Customer Satisfaction Index (ACSI). Reichheld asserted that the ACSI was examined and found to have a 0.00 correlation to growth.[33] (A zero correlation means that there is absolutely no connection to growth whatsoever.) Therefore, our examination should have given every advantage to NPS.

The results of our investigation, however, unambiguously proved that the claims of NPS's superiority were false. The left side of Figure 1.2 shows the NPS charts presented in *The Ultimate Question*. For the charts on the right, we simply substituted the ACSI levels for NPS for the same time periods. Surprisingly, the ACSI tended to perform better despite the fact that these same charts were presented as prime examples of the strength of the NPS-growth relationship.

It is important to note that these charts do not prove that either the ACSI or NPS are strong predictors of growth. These examples simply allowed us to test the claims of superiority by comparing the original NPS data with the ACSI. In fact, there were serious problems with using this method as evidence of a relationship to growth. The growth rates presented in *The Ultimate Question* included time periods that occurred before the NPS time frames (in other words, the linkage was to the past, not the future). As a result, it does not represent a valid test of the relationship between the ACSI or NPS and business growth. That requires a rigorous scientific investigation, which looks at firms in numerous industries over time.

Fortunately, as noted earlier, that has already been done—several times—by leading academic researchers and reported in some of the best peer-reviewed scientific journals. The results from all of these studies find the same poor relationship to growth. To quote professors Van Doorn, Leeflang, and Tijs, "We find that all metrics perform ... equally poor for predicting future sales growth and gross margins as well as current and future net cash flows.... The predictive capability of customer metrics, such as NPS, for future company growth rates is limited."[34]

Now we explain why this is so.

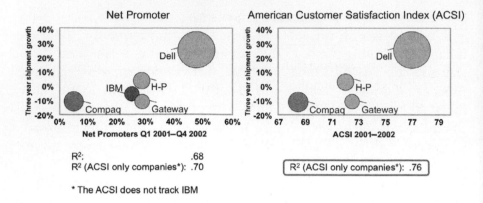

R²: .68
R² (ACSI only companies*): .70

R² (ACSI only companies*): .76

* The ACSI does not track IBM

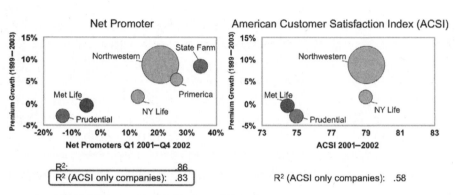

R²: .86
R² (ACSI only companies): .83

R² (ACSI only companies): .58

* The ACSI does not track Primerica and State Farm

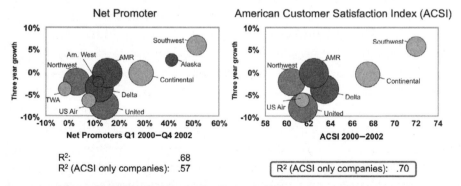

R²: .68
R² (ACSI only companies): .57

R² (ACSI only companies): .70

* The ACSI does not track Alaska, Am. West, and TWA

FIGURE 1.2 A Comparison of Net Promoter Score and the American Customer Satisfaction Index Using Net Promoter Data from the Book *The Ultimate Question*

Satisfaction ≠ Market Share

The empirical association between a firm's market share and the (mean) satisfaction of its customers is not positive.... Not a single company with a market share above 30 percent could be said to have high customer satisfaction. All firms with higher levels of satisfaction also had lower market shares.[35]

—Professor Claes Fornell regarding his examination of the Swedish Customer Satisfaction Index

Most managers believe that higher satisfaction and NPS levels are associated with higher market share levels. CEOs and boards of directors are so convinced of this that it has become quite common to base employees' compensation in part on achieving targeted customer satisfaction levels.

The unfortunate reality for managers betting on satisfaction, however, is quite the opposite. For most sectors, the relationship between companies' customer satisfaction/NPS levels and their market shares is negative. In other words, higher company (or brand) satisfaction/NPS levels tend to correspond to lower market share.

The first reaction of most managers to this fact is disbelief. After all, the press is filled with articles from consultants and business pundits that purport to show how improving satisfaction/NPS leads to amazing market share success. Although we have no doubt that these pundits can point to examples of firms that grew while increasing their satisfaction/NPS scores (just as every miracle weight loss cure has testimonials to support their claims), the data supporting a negative relationship are too overwhelming to deny.

In fact, we see examples of this negative relationship all the time. We simply don't pay attention to it because it doesn't correspond to what we expect to see. Regardless, it is quite literally staring us in the face.

Think for a moment about the big three burger chains in the United States. McDonald's consistently ranks below Burger King and Wendy's in customer satisfaction. For 17 of the 18 years that the ACSI has tracked these firms, Wendy's has always had the highest satisfaction level, Burger King has been second, and McDonald's has ranked third. Despite its

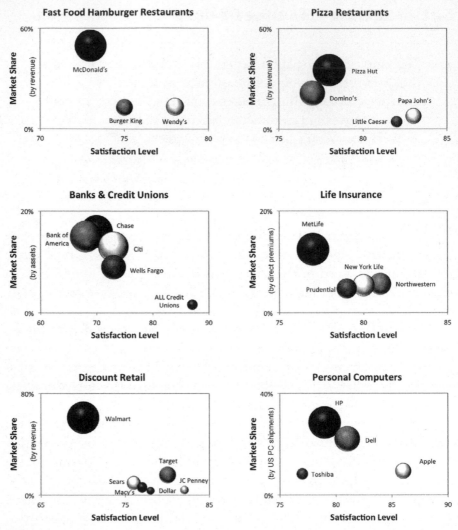

FIGURE 1.3 The Relationship between Satisfaction and Market Share Is Often Negative
Satisfaction levels from the American Customer Satisfaction Index

consistent last place satisfaction levels among the big three, however, McDonald's has by far the largest market share (see Figure 1.3).

The story is similar in retail. Since 2007, Walmart has recorded the lowest customer satisfaction scores of all discount retailers tracked by the ACSI. Target, Sears, and JCPenney all consistently outperform Walmart on customer satisfaction year after year. Despite low relative satisfaction levels, however, Walmart has a dominant market share. In fact, outside of the U.S. Department of Defense and China's People's Liberation Army, Walmart is the largest employer in the world.[36]

The negative satisfaction–market share relationship also holds true in financial services. For example, MetLife has significantly lower satisfaction than its main competitors for life insurance but has substantially greater market share. And in retail banking, larger banks have substantially lower satisfaction levels than their regional bank and credit union competitors but far greater market share. In fact, credit unions have achieved the highest customer satisfaction level of any industry investigated by the ACSI[37] yet they hold correspondingly very low market shares relative to their big bank competitors.[38]

The reality is that satisfaction is not a predictor of market share. However, market share is a strong negative predictor of future customer satisfaction.[39] So for firms with high market share levels (or goals of attaining high levels), a focus on high satisfaction is not compatible.

The primary reason for this seemingly counterintuitive finding is that the broader a company's market appeal relative to the offerings of competitors, the lower the level of satisfaction. Why? Gaining market share typically comes from attracting customers whose needs are not completely aligned with the company's core target market. As a result, on the one hand, smaller niche firms are better able to serve their customers (see Figure 1.4). Large market share firms, on the other hand, must by their very nature serve a more diverse set of customers. The more diverse the customer base, the less likely that a firm's offering will meet a customer's ideal—hence, satisfaction will be lower. Yet because of their appeal to a broader group of customers, these firms generate higher market share than their smaller niche competitors.

The fact that firms with more similar customer bases tend to have higher satisfaction provides managers with another uncomfortable reality. Customer satisfaction ratings can increase as a result of a decline in market share. For example, an examination of the ACSI shows that Burger King's satisfaction levels rose over the same time period that it was losing share to McDonald's and Wendy's, dropping it from the second- to the third-largest fast food burger chain. Similarly, Kmart scored its biggest year-over-year increase in customer satisfaction (and its highest ACSI score since tracking for the firm began) as it was preparing its bankruptcy filing as a result of large-scale customer defections. The reason for this is that when customers are defecting, the customers that remain typically like the firm or brand—if they didn't, they would leave as well.

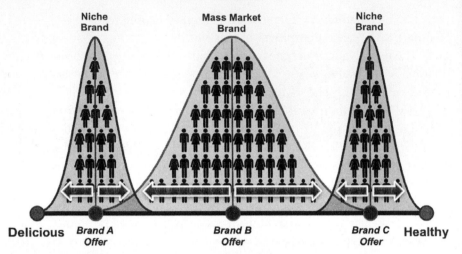

FIGURE 1.4 Mass Market Brands versus Niche Brands
Mass market brands have lower satisfaction scores than niche brands. They also have a wider dispersion of customers—and as a result, many don't receive their ideal offer. Niche brands must appeal to a small, more homogeneous group to survive.

All of us have also experienced another common cause of the negative relationship between satisfaction and market share in some industries. Specifically, busy places often mean more headaches. Virtually all of us have been to stores where the lines were so long that you could feel yourself age while waiting to pay for your items and leave. As a result, large retailers often see a negative relationship between their stores' sales and their corresponding satisfaction levels (see Figure 1.5). Of course, no manager recommends reducing the number of customers who come into the store to improve satisfaction. Unfortunately for these high-sales store managers, their stores are typically expected to achieve the same satisfaction levels as their less busy sister stores.

Given that brands with larger market share are likely to have lower satisfaction than smaller brands, how exactly are managers to compare their performance vis-à-vis competition? In our own experience, managers of some the world's largest brands often benchmark their performance against the highest satisfaction brands in the category despite the fact that their share is often significantly smaller. Moreover, senior executives tend to view these levels as attainable targets for their own firms given that they were achieved by a competitor.

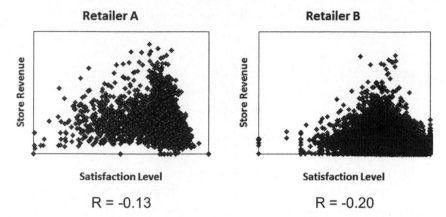

FIGURE 1.5 For Many Retailers, the Relationship between Store-Level Satisfaction and Revenue Is Negative

Each point in the chart represents an individual store within a particular brand. The y-axis shows the revenue for a particular store, and the x-axis shows its corresponding satisfaction level. A negative correlation in this case indicates that store size (based on revenue) and satisfaction are negatively related—in other words, higher revenue is associated with lower satisfaction.

Consultants often go even farther down this path. It is virtually impossible for managers to go through their employment histories without hearing a management guru expound on how their brands should be more like the great but niche brands of Harley Davidson, Disney, Cirque du Soleil, and so on. The underlying argument is that customer expectations are set not only by the performance of direct competitors but by all firms with which customers conduct business. Although there may be a grain of truth to this argument, most of the time it is not managerially relevant. It is good to learn from the experiences of other firms, but setting target satisfaction levels based on the performance of niche players isn't just unrealistic; it's a bad business decision. If the goal is market share, pursuing the highest satisfaction levels is not a compatible strategy!

Satisfaction ≠ Share of Wallet

When is the ultimate customer-service-measurement number not enough? That's what Jiffy Lube asked recently when the company discovered that its Net Promoter Scores—a popular customer-service metric known as the "one number you need to grow"—weren't actually helping it grow.... One of the initial head-scratching finds was that the overall NPS rating had almost no correlation to return visits. That meant customers who said they'd gladly recommend Jiffy Lube to friends didn't necessarily return to the store themselves.[40]

—Ad Age

It is easy to understand why managers expect customers' satisfaction and NPS levels to be strongly linked to the share of category spending that customers allocate to the brands that they use. Unfortunately, it is not even remotely true.

Without a doubt, numerous scientific studies show that there is indeed a *statistically* significant positive relationship between satisfaction and customers' purchasing behaviors.[41] Unfortunately, there is a problem with this relationship: Although it is *statistically* significant, it most definitely is not *managerially* significant.

Managers tend to misunderstand the concept of statistical significance. In everyday English, *significant* means "important." In statistics, however, it means "probably not a random occurrence." The problem for managers is that many things can be significant in the statistical sense without being important. That's definitely the case with the relationship between satisfaction and customers' purchasing behaviors. In fact, the relationship is so extraordinarily weak that it is managerially irrelevant.

This is not an overstatement. Satisfaction (and NPS) is so weakly correlated with the share of spending that customers allocate to the brands that they use that it is useless as a metric to drive higher share of wallet.

This naturally raises the question, "Exactly how weak is the relationship?" In our examination of the relationship between satisfaction/NPS and share of wallet, we reviewed more than 250,000 consumer ratings covering in excess of 650 brands from more than a dozen countries; we found that the average variance explained is around 1 percent.[42] In layman's terms, this means that 99 percent of what is going on with consumers' share of category spending is completely unexplained by knowing their satisfaction level or NPS. Worse still, the effect of the change in satisfaction on changes in share of wallet is even weaker. Our research finds that changes in satisfaction (and NPS) explain a miniscule 0.4 percent of the change in share of wallet over time.[43]

Given that managers measure and manage satisfaction levels and NPS because they are thought to link to growth, this is disastrous. When the relationship is this weak, there is no reliable way to predict financial outcomes from improving satisfaction and NPS.

Most managers don't want to accept this reality. In fact, we are often challenged by managers on this. Fortunately for us, it is very easy for managers to see this for themselves using simple spreadsheet software such as Microsoft Excel.

If your firm is collecting satisfaction and/or NPS data, simply create a spreadsheet containing customers' satisfaction and share of wallet data. Specifically, input customers' satisfaction ratings (or NPS classifications) for your firm or brand in one column and their share of wallet in another (see Figure 1.6). Now all you have to do is determine how much of the

	A	B	C
1	Customer ID	Satisfaction	Share of Wallet
2	1	9	30%
3	2	8	60%
4	3	7	15%
5	4	9	75%
998	997	10	35%
999	998	9	45%
1000	999	8	25%
1001	1000	8	50%
1002			
1003		R-square	1.13%

FIGURE 1.6 It Is Easy to Prove that Satisfaction and NPS Are Very Weak Predictors of Share of Wallet

It is easy for managers to see for themselves that the correlation between satisfaction/NPS and share of wallet is very weak by using simple spreadsheet software such as Microsoft Excel. Simply input customers' satisfaction (or NPS) levels for your firm or brand in one column, and their corresponding share of category spending (share of wallet) in another column. Then compute the R-square, the squared correlation coefficient. The percentage of variance explained (i.e., R-square) is almost always less than 5 percent and is typically around 1 percent.

Note 1: In Microsoft Excel the formula for calculating R-square is =RSQ(column1,column2). Columns 1 and 2 correspond to customers' satisfaction and share of wallet levels—when computing R-square it does not matter whether satisfaction is column 1 or column 2 in the Microsoft Excel formula.

Note 2: If you are using the Net Promoter Score, simply input "3" for Promoters, "2" for Passives, and "1" for Detractors.

variance in share of wallet is explained by knowing satisfaction levels or NPS. This is done by computing what is called the R-square. Fortunately, this isn't difficult to do. Microsoft Excel provides a simple function to compute the R-square, so there is no complicated mathematics necessary to find out how strongly your satisfaction/NPS metric links to your customers' share of spending with your brand.

Doing this always results in bad news. The percentage of variance explained will almost always be less than 5 percent—typically around 1 percent—meaning that 95 percent or more of the variation in your customers' spending is completely unexplained by the satisfaction or NPS metric your firm is tracking.

Always Wrong on Average

Given that it is so easy to prove that customers' satisfaction and NPS levels have virtually no meaningful correlation to share of wallet, why is it that managers overwhelming believe that they do?

The most important reason is that we *want* to believe. It fits our sense of how the world *should* work. We want to believe that more satisfied customers allocate a greater share of their spending than less satisfied customers.

Research and consulting firms have fed this belief by presenting misleading information about the relationship between customer satisfaction and spending. For example, virtually every manager has seen or heard something similar to the following: On average, promoters/delighted customers spend $X more than detractors/dissatisfied customers (see Figure 1.7).

To be clear, we have no doubt that the averages presented by consultants and researchers are correct. They are just irrelevant. Because satisfaction and NPS do such a poor job of explaining customers' spending levels, using satisfaction and NPS levels to group customers does not meaningfully explain why one group spends more than another.

Average levels are a means of gauging the center of a distribution of people. As a result, in calculating the average, both positive and negative extremes cancel each other out (see Figure 1.8).

To get a better idea as to why this is misleading, instead of thinking about satisfaction and spending, think about peoples' weight and the

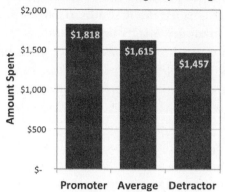

Satisfaction and Average Spending Among Fans vs. Non-Fans

	👍 Fans	👎 Non-Fans
$ Average Spend	$255	$139

FIGURE 1.7 Examples of Reported Higher Average Spending levels for one group versus another based on satisfaction, Net Promoter Score, and liking levels

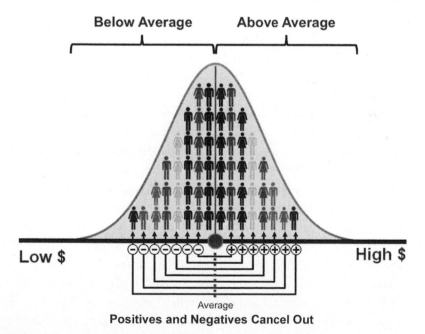

FIGURE 1.8 Averages Can Be Misleading because Positive and Negative Values Cancel Out

regions in which they live. Let's assume that people in the northern part of the country weigh more on average than people in the southern part of the country. Let's also presume that the difference is statistically significant.

Even though this information is true, it doesn't help very much in gauging the weight of any individual. In fact, if you were provided with only the weight of each individual in the country, you would not be able to accurately predict whether they lived in the northern or southern part of the country.

This is because there is a huge dispersion in the weight of individuals within each region of the country. As a result, there will be a tremendous overlap of people with the same weight (above and below average) in both the north and the south.

The same problem happens with using satisfaction levels and NPS to distinguish customer spending patterns (see Figure 1.9). Although the average may be higher for each group, the overlap is so great that it is managerially irrelevant.

Another, less obvious way that researchers and consultants misleadingly use satisfaction and NPS levels is through the use of firm-level averages (as was done in Figure 1.2). This is especially problematic when these firm-level averages are correlated to metrics based on individual customer behaviors, such as share of category spending, sales, and so on.

For example, in our research we found that firm-level satisfaction for U.S. banks and credit unions was highly correlated to the average share of deposits customers held with the various financial institutions that they used.[44] The problem was that at the individual customer level, satisfaction was very weakly correlated to share of deposits.

Because managers are trained to benchmark their firm's performance relative to that of competitors, these firm-level analyses can appear very persuasive. Unfortunately, most managers are unaware that correlations at the aggregate level are typically much higher than at the individual level. As was shown in Figure 1.8, this occurs because positive and negative extremes at the individual level cancel themselves out at the group level.

Therefore, firm-level correlations that differ dramatically from individual-level correlations should be treated with suspicion. In fact, there are actually statistical rules for when you are allowed to aggregate data.[45] A simple rule of thumb is that you are never allowed to aggregate data when the relationship between the variable you are tracking and the outcome variable is very weak.

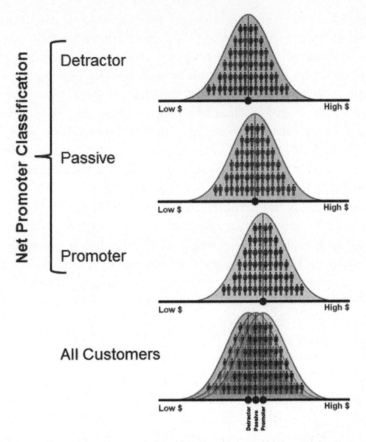

FIGURE 1.9 Averages Based on Satisfaction and NPS Levels Do Not Accurately Reflect Spending Differences by Individuals within Each Group

The customer-level relationship between your metric of choice (e.g., satisfaction, recommend intention, NPS classifications of promoter, passive, or detractor) and share of wallet must first strongly link *before* you can aggregate the data. If this is not the case, the use of aggregate-level data will most likely result in what researchers call the *ecological fallacy*.[46] Specifically, an aggregate-level correlation is incorrectly assumed to apply at the individual level.

An overly simplified example should help demonstrate the problem of the ecological fallacy. In 2011, *National Geographic* produced a video designed to show the world's most "typical" person.[47] What *National Geographic* found is that the typical person is a 28-year-old Chinese man who makes less than $12,000 per year and has a cell phone but not a bank account. Although that insight makes for fun trivia, it clearly isn't very useful when thinking about the best way to understand the needs and wants of individuals, because people vary dramatically from the average.

For group-level information to be managerially relevant, the individuals within the group need to reflect the average—otherwise, the average gives wrong information about the people within the group. Therefore, when presented with averages (e.g., the average promoter spends $X), managers need to insist that their research partners provide them with the individual-level correlations corresponding to these averages so that they can gauge the usefulness of this information.

The good news is that individual-level correlations from a firm's customer research are typically very easy for researchers to provide. Furthermore, because research professionals and consultants know (or should know) about the ecological fallacy, they should want to minimize the possibility that managers will draw incorrect conclusions from their research. Regardless, it is management's responsibility to insist that they do.

A Cautionary Tale

The fact that satisfaction does not link to customers' share of category spending has huge implications for managers. Managers typically survey customers to gauge their experience via metrics such as satisfaction, recommendation intention, and purchase intention. The underlying logic is that there is a virtuous chain of effects that lead from positive customer perceptions of product/service performance to share of wallet, specifically product/service performance → satisfaction/intentions → share of wallet. For that reason, managers identify those aspects of the product/service experience that most strongly affect these metrics as primary targets for improvement in the belief that this will ultimately result in improved share of wallet.

Without question, the logic is intuitive. . . . It also doesn't work!

The result is that companies spend a great deal of time and money on efforts to improve customers' perceptions of the experience, but typically they find that the impact on customers' share of spending shows very little improvement. To see the danger of this situation, one need only look to the biggest company on the planet, Walmart.

During the Great Recession of 2008, Walmart was one of a very few retailers seeing same-store sales increases. Most other retailers, including

Walmart and Target Year Over Year Change in Same Store Sales

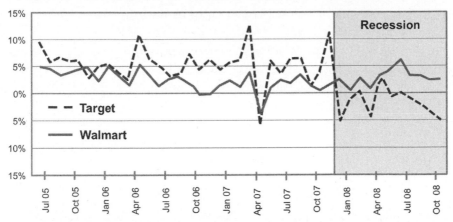

FIGURE 1.10 Walmart Performed Consistently Well during the Recession of 2008 While Most Retailers Saw Sales Declines

its rival Target, saw significant same-store sales declines over this same period (see Figure 1.10).

With competitors reeling from the recession, Walmart embarked on a new initiative to "crush the competition," to quote *Time* magazine.[48] Dubbed Project Impact, it represented a dramatic remodeling initiative designed to improve the customer experience based on extensive customer feedback. Despite consistent sales performance over time, the one area in which Walmart significantly lagged its competitors was customer satisfaction. Project Impact was going to change that and crush the competition in the process.

As a result, the familiar pallets in the aisles stacked high with items disappeared. Displays at the ends of aisles were reduced. And the dizzying array of merchandise jammed on the shelves was streamlined so as not to overwhelm customers.

The good news was that it had a very positive effect on customers' perceptions of shopping at Walmart. In fact, Walmart reported that because of Project Impact, customer satisfaction jumped to an all-time high.[49]

Unfortunately, the launch of Project Impact resulted in the one of the longest same-store sales declines in the company's history (see Figure 1.11). Higher customer satisfaction actually resulted in customers allocating a lower share of their spending to Walmart.

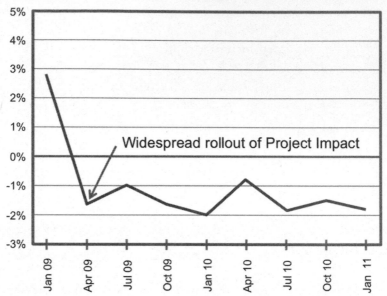

Walmart Year Over Year Change in Same Store Sales

FIGURE 1.11   The Launch of Project Impact Began One of the Longest Same Store Sales Declines in Walmart's History

To be clear, the problem wasn't that customers stopped shopping at Walmart. "The customer, for the most part, is still in the store shopping," observes Charles Holley, Walmart's Chief Financial Officer, "but they started doing some more shopping elsewhere."[50]

Moreover, the loss in sales was not the result of a bad economy. Competitors like Target and Dollar Stores enjoyed strong same-store sales growth during this same time period.[51]

The reason for the decline in sales rested squarely on the rollout of Project Impact.[52] The effort cost Walmart $2 billion—enough revenue to qualify as a Fortune 1000 company. The executive behind Project Impact is now an ex-Walmart employee, and his team has been effectively disbanded.[53]

Project Impact shows the danger of focusing on improving customer satisfaction absent a strong linkage to customer spending. To quote William S. Simon, CEO of Walmart's U.S. division, "They loved the experience. They just bought less. And that generally is not a good long-term strategy."

The Moral of the Story?

Without question, no firm can last for very long without satisfied customers. But a misguided focus on improving satisfaction and NPS levels is a recipe for financial disaster.

There is no getting around the fact that satisfaction and NPS levels have almost no correlation to the share of category spending that customers give to your brand. Please, don't take our word for it—prove it for yourself using simple spreadsheet software (as was shown in Figure 1.6). Without a strong linkage between satisfaction/NPS levels and customers' share of spending, there is virtually no way to make efforts to improve satisfaction and NPS pay off.

Equally damning, if the goal is market share leadership, then pursuing satisfaction leadership is not compatible. In fact, to gain market share, managers need to accept lower satisfaction levels by appealing to a larger, more diverse customer base.

This contradicts the message of virtually all programs discussed in the business press regarding the relationship of satisfaction and NPS levels to business performance. The grim reality is that most of these efforts are doomed to fail. Moreover, they often run counter to a firm's competitive positioning and strategy.

Although the current situation is grim, it doesn't have to be. These issues are solvable. But they won't be solved by continuing to do what's always been done, only better. It requires new ways of looking at the problem. More important, it requires a willingness to let go of legacy systems that don't work.

That's hard. Many managers have put their reputations on the line in support of these systems. Some have even reported flawed linkages to customer spending—of course, the corresponding growth in sales that would be expected from such a linkage rarely materializes.

What is even harder, however, will be facing competitors willing to make the change. They will be able to accurately identify what it really takes to drive customers' spending with their brands. They will make the right calls to drive market share.

As a result, change will happen. In the end, the truth will win. And the truth is that the current situation is "Oh my God!" bad.

Eureka! The Discovery of the Wallet Allocation Rule

The greatest obstacle to discovery is not ignorance. It is the illusion of knowledge.[1]

—*Daniel J. Boorstin, Pulitzer Prize-winning historian*

"Satisfaction guaranteed or your money back!" Montgomery Ward—the inventor of the general merchandise mail order catalog—began using this promise in 1875 to differentiate its mail order catalog from other retailers.[2] It has become the standard promise of almost every business around the world.

Montgomery Ward recognized that the only way for his business to survive and grow was to build a foundation of satisfied customers. It's just good business. In fact, it is a core component of economic theory. An underlying principle of economics—referred to as Gossen's second law—states: "a person maximizes his utility when he distributes his available money among the various goods so that he obtains the same amount of *satisfaction* from the last unit of money spent upon each commodity."[3]

This idea is so ingrained in our daily lives that it seems self-evident—people buy more from places that do a better job of satisfying them. Moreover, a lot of researchers (including us) have provided scientific evidence that confirms a statistically significant relationship between customer satisfaction and customer spending.[4]

But the problem is that while a statistically significant relationship exists, the strength of that relationship is so incredibly weak that it is managerially irrelevant. As a result, it is almost impossible for managers to meaningfully connect their efforts to improve satisfaction with tangible financial outcomes.

Not surprisingly, this weak (almost nonexistent) relationship hasn't gone unnoticed. The result has been a wave of skepticism and in some cases outright disdain by managers and consultants toward customer satisfaction measurement and management. Books such as *Customer Satisfaction Is Worthless, Customer Loyalty Is Priceless* by noted sales training consultant Jeffrey Gitomer point to the frustration that managers experience when they try to make customer experience pay back financially. In fact, the Net Promoter Score (NPS) came into existence precisely because of this frustration: "Not only is Net Promoter Score a simpler, more easily understood, and more actionable measure than customer-satisfaction ratings, but it also links directly to the economics of growth."[5]

Unfortunately, the reported NPS linkage failed to stand up to scrutiny, with all major scientific investigations showing a very poor relationship to growth.[6] This is not surprising given that the correlation between a customer's NPS level and his or her share of wallet is extraordinarily weak.

Given that share of category spending (aka share of wallet) is the most important demonstration of customers' loyalty to a firm or brand and that traditional metrics don't link well with share of wallet, there is an obvious problem with how we currently measure and manage customer loyalty. This reality forced us to do some serious soul-searching. If there were no way to meaningfully link how customers feel about the brands or firms they use and the way they allocate their spending, then the overriding reason for focusing on the customer experience is wrong. And if it is wrong, then we had to find out why.

This led us to conduct a comprehensive investigation to uncover why satisfaction and other commonly used metrics do not link to the share of spending that customers allocate to the brands they use. Our overriding goals were to determine (1) the best approach to link customer metrics with share of wallet and (2) the best metric for managers to track.

What we found shocked us. Our research uncovered a heretofore unknown relationship between customers' perceptions of the brands they use and their share of wallet that could be easily calculated using a simple mathematical formula, the Wallet Allocation Rule formula:

$$Share\ of\ wallet = \left(1 - \frac{rank}{number\ of\ brands + 1} \right) \times \left(\frac{2}{number\ of\ brands} \right)$$

where:

Rank $=$ the relative position that a customer assigns to a brand in comparison to other brands also used by the customer in the category

Number of brands $=$ the total number of brands used in the category by the customer

The ramifications of the Wallet Allocation Rule are profound. Using this simple formula, managers can easily and strongly link their customer metrics with share of wallet. From company to company, and industry to industry, the correlation between the Wallet Allocation Rule and customers' share of wallet was remarkably strong. Even more important, the correlation between changes in the Wallet Allocation Rule score and changes in share of wallet was also strong.

Many readers are likely very skeptical. After all, quite literally thousands of researchers have examined customer satisfaction data for almost half a century. Furthermore, we have been burned before—every other highly touted new metric has failed to link to customers' spending behaviors.

We understand that skepticism. In fact, when we first discovered the Wallet Allocation Rule, we didn't shout "Eureka!" We said, "That can't possibly be right."

But after having put the Wallet Allocation Rule through numerous, rigorous scientific investigations, we know it works.

Getting There

The discovery of the Wallet Allocation Rule was made by a team of leading academics and industry experts with the goal of bringing the best of the science and practice together. Most important, the team wasn't just capable of doing a rigorous analysis. Its members were willing to go wherever the results led them—even if that meant contradicting things they had advocated in the past.

The first step was to critically rethink the nature of the relationship between customer satisfaction and customer spending. Beliefs that could not be supported with hard data were discarded. The team then compared what was proved to be true with how customer satisfaction is currently measured and managed. Surprisingly, despite decades of scientific research into customer satisfaction, two serious disconnects between what researchers and managers know to be true and what is actually done were discovered.

Issue 1: Satisfaction Is Relative to Competitive Alternatives, but That Is Not Reflected in How We Measure Satisfaction

Every manager knows that customer satisfaction is relative to the other firms or brands a customer uses. You would never know this, however, from the way companies gauge their customers' satisfaction levels. Typically, managers focus on the absolute satisfaction scores. For example, a customer who gives a rating of 9 or 10 (where 10 is the highest and 0 is the lowest rating level possible) regarding her likelihood to recommend the firm is classified as a promoter using the NPS process, regardless of how that customer feels about other brands she uses in the category.

Issue 2: A Company's Market Share Is Strongly Linked to Its Relative Rank vis-à-vis Competition, but This Insight Has Been of Little Practical Value to Managers

Scientific researchers have known for some time that market share is related to rank.[7] In other words, if you are provided with the number of firms in an industry and told their relative rank (e.g., which firm was first, second, third, etc., in market share), you could do a pretty good job estimating the market shares of each of the firms in the category using a simple mathematical formula.

Most managers are not even aware that such a relationship exists. Even if they did, virtually all managers would have no idea how to use this in the day-to-day management of their businesses. But it has serious implications for companies. If rank and share are linked, then this means that companies are unlikely to make significant gains in market share by inching their way up the market share curve. Because a particular rank is associated with a particular market share, this implies that to significantly gain share, a firm needs to occupy a different rank vis-à-vis its competitors.

Putting It Together

These two seemingly unrelated issues—(1) satisfaction is relative, and (2) rank matters—are actually integrally related to one another. Regarding issue 1 (satisfaction is relative), the underlying problem is that it is not the absolute "score" that a customer assigns that matters—it is a customer's *perception of performance* relative to competitive alternatives. Regarding issue 2 (rank and market share are linked), rank is a means of gauging relative position vis-à-vis competitive alternatives.

To see how these issues relate to one another, imagine that your brand has two customers: Janet and John (see Figure 2.1). Both Janet and John rate their satisfaction with your brand a 9 on a 10-point scale (where 10 is the highest level of satisfaction). Nearly all managers would consider this a good score. Using the NPS classification system, both Janet and John would be considered promoters.

Janet and John, however, also use two other brands: *Brand A* and *Brand B*. On the one hand, Janet rates her level of satisfaction with *Brand A* a 9 and her satisfaction with *Brand B* a 10. On the other hand, John rates his level of satisfaction with *Brand A* a 7 and with *Brand B* an 8.

Your Customer	Satisfaction ---- Rank	Your Brand	Competitors		Share of Wallet
			A	B	
Janet	Sat.	9	9	10	**25%**
	Rank	(2.5)	2.5	1	
John	Sat.	9	7	8	**50%**
	Rank	(1)	3	2	

FIGURE 2.1 Different Ranks Result in Different Wallet Shares

Despite the fact that Janet and John both rate your brand a 9, with John your brand is his clear first choice. With Janet, your brand is tied for last. The result of this difference in rank is that John allocates a substantially higher share of his category spending with your brand than Janet does.

This problem happens all the time. For most industries, customers divide their spending in the category among multiple competing brands. But not all brands are equal in satisfying customers. We would naturally expect preferred brands to get a greater share of customers' spending in the category. Relative "ranked" satisfaction levels easily capture these preferences. As a result, they are more strongly related to share of wallet than the absolute score given to each firm. In fact, our research found that simply transforming absolute satisfaction levels to relative ranks tended to explain more than 20 percent of the variation in customers' share of category spending.[8] This is a remarkable improvement given that absolute satisfaction levels tend to explain only 1 percent of the variation in share of wallet.

Determining Your Rank

Given that rank is far superior to absolute satisfaction levels in linking to share of wallet, the next logical question is, "What's the best way to determine rank?" The seemingly obvious answer—simply to ask customers to rank the firms they use—turns out not to be the best solution. If you simply ask people to rank things from best to worst, they will forcibly assign a distinct rank (first, second, third, etc.) for each item.

The problem is that these distinct ranks are not how customers typically view the brands they use. Although a customer may have a clear favorite brand he uses, chances are he also uses several brands that he views as being the same. Therefore, having customers force brands into distinct ranks does not reflect their actual perception of these brands.

So it is important to make it easy for there to be ties. Researchers have found that a good way to do this is to rescale customers' ratings of the brands they use into ranks. Most important, this process makes it possible to link the data collected in customer surveys with customers' actual purchase behaviors.

Given that ties are important, the issue then becomes how to account for ties. In most of the rankings we see—sporting events, school rankings, and so on—a tie means that everyone who achieved the same level gets to share the highest rank. In other words, it's possible for more than one team to legitimately say, "We're number one!"

When it comes to customers' share of wallet allocations, though, there are no multiple gold medal winners. If two brands are tied for first place with a customer, neither brand gets the rewards that would accrue if one brand were the sole winner. After all, the size of the customer's wallet doesn't change because several of the brands he uses are tied.

Instead, rewards are divided evenly among tied competitors for the places they would have occupied had they not been tied. So if two brands are tied for first place, they would have occupied spots 1 and 2. As a result, their rank would correspond to 1.5. The next potential rank, assuming no other ties, would be 3 (i.e., third place).

The Wallet Allocation Rule and Share: The Evidence

We embarked on an extensive investigation to see if our belief about the relationship between rank and share of wallet was correct. We surveyed more than 5,500 customers across a dozen industries, collecting customers' satisfaction and loyalty ratings across a wide array of questions. In addition, we obtained a purchase history for each person surveyed. We then examined the data to see if any relationship actually existed between the customer metrics we collected and share of wallet.

What we discovered was quite unexpected. Not only was there a relationship between rank and share of wallet, but it followed a clear pattern that can be predicted by two things: a brand's rank among competitors used and the number of brands used (see Figure 2.2). Most important, this prediction could be calculated using a very simple mathematical formula—the Wallet Allocation Rule.

The correlations between share of wallet and the Wallet Allocation Rule across the industries investigated were remarkable (see Figure 2.3). More important, both the customer-level and the firm-level correlations were strong. These findings indicated that it was possible to predict share of wallet with a high degree of accuracy by simply knowing the rank and the number of brands used by the customer.

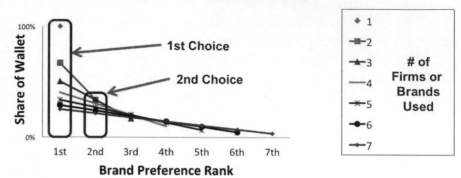

Share of Wallet
by Firm/Brand Preference and Number of Competitors

FIGURE 2.2 The Relationship between Rank and Share of Wallet Follows a Clear Pattern

The relationship between a firm's/brand's rank and share of wallet can be predicted by two things: relative ranking of firm/brand used by a customer and number of firms/brands used by a customer.

Rather than celebrate this discovery, however, we needed to be sure we were right. After all, many seemingly great initial discoveries have failed under the real-world demands of business competition.

When we began this investigation, we expected that finding a strong relationship would require a complex mathematical formula filled with Greek symbols. The Wallet Allocation Rule, however, is so simple that it was hard for us to accept that we were the first to discover it (particularly given the thousands of researchers who examine satisfaction data all the time).

Given our skepticism, we insisted upon rigorous testing of our findings. First, we needed to be confident that the Wallet Allocation Rule would work across cultures. We therefore surveyed more than 7,000 customers in eight non–North American countries (covering four continents) about their usage of credit cards. We selected this industry to minimize the likelihood that industry structure and the uniqueness of competitors in the various countries would significantly influence our results. Our investigation found strong correlations between the Wallet Allocation Rule and share of wallet for all countries examined.

Although these results were impressive, we needed to be certain that the Wallet Allocation Rule would reveal consistent results over time and prove to be a useful key performance indicator for managers to track.

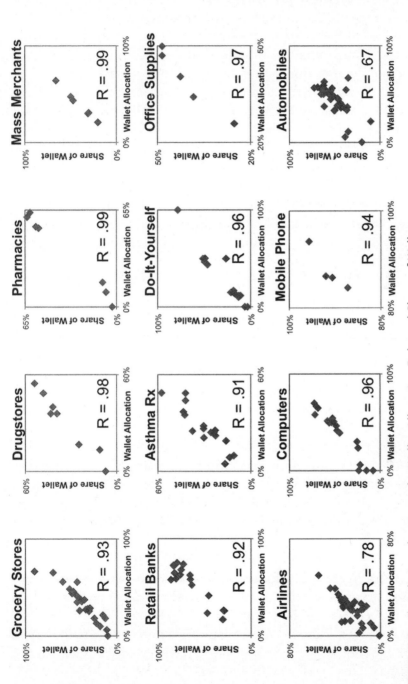

FIGURE 2.3 Correlations between the Wallet Allocation Rule and Share of Wallet

Note: Scatter diagrams show the average share of wallet at the firm/brand level (y-axis) by the predicted average share of wallet using the Wallet Allocation Rule (x-axis).

Specifically, we needed to be certain that changes in Wallet Allocation Rule scores corresponded to changes in share of wallet over time.

That need, however, presented us with a challenge. It was unreasonable to expect large shifts in customer metrics and share of wallet levels just a few months after completing our initial wave of surveys.

Instead, we needed to examine markets in which customers' share of wallet allocations were changing rapidly. This meant something disruptive had to have happened within a market. The difficulty from a research perspective is that we had to know exactly when this disruption would take place to ensure that we could measure share of wallet before and after the event.

To address this problem, we examined markets in which a new retail store was scheduled to open. Clearly, the opening of a new store dramatically disrupts competitive dynamics in a market area, quickly shifting customers' spending patterns.

We studied two different retail markets covering two distinct product categories, before and after the opening of new stores. The results of this test demonstrated a strong link between the Wallet Allocation Rule and share of wallet regardless of changes in market dynamics and corresponding shifts in customers' share of category spending.

We also went back to five of the eight countries examined regarding credit card usage after approximately six months. The results between the two waves of data were essentially identical, all demonstrating strong correlations.

The most important test had yet to come, though. We needed to know if changes in an individual customer's share of wallet matched changes predicted by the Wallet Allocation Rule. To do this, we had to do something rarely done in customer satisfaction research. Approximately one year after our initial investigation, we went back to the same customers to find out.

The results unambiguously demonstrate that the Wallet Allocation Rule links strongly to individual customer behavior (see Figure 2.4). By comparison, changes in other commonly used metrics show a very weak correlation to changes in share of wallet.

The findings of this research were published in the *Harvard Business Review*.[9] One month later, the research received the Next Gen Market Research Award for Disruptive Innovation.[10]

Next we sought to replicate these findings through a large-scale study of the U.S. credit union and retail banking market.[11] In a survey of 4,712

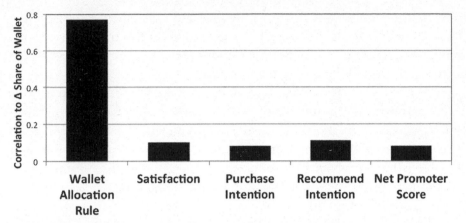

FIGURE 2.4 Changes in the Wallet Allocation Rule Score Are Strongly Correlated to Changes in Customers' Share of Wallet Allocations Over Time The figure shows the correlation between the change in individual customers' share of wallet allocations over time and the predicted change in share of wallet based on the Wallet Allocation Rule and other commonly used satisfaction and loyalty metrics.

banking customers across the country, we found that the Wallet Allocation Rule explained 55 percent of the variation in customers' share of deposits. (*Share of deposits* refers to the percentage of deposits that a customer allocates with a particular financial institution.) By contrast, common metrics such as satisfaction and NPS level explained less than 10 percent. The findings of this study were published in the *International Journal of Bank Marketing,* a peer-reviewed academic journal in the field of financial services marketing.[12]

Finally, we sought to replicate our findings using a large-scale, multicountry database and a team of leading academic researchers from Northwestern, Vanderbilt, Fordham, and Ghent Universities. We examined 79,543 customers who provided 258,743 satisfaction ratings regarding the brands they use within a particular industry covering more than 650 brands from 22 industries and in 15 countries.

In this investigation, we conducted a comprehensive comparison of the Wallet Allocation Rule and multiple alternative approaches that have either been proposed by other researchers or represent logical choices for comparison based on prior scientific studies. The models were examined using multiple performance criteria. Again, the Wallet Allocation Rule was found to perform as well as other, more complex models in linking to share of wallet. In fact, the absolute correlation between a change in the Wallet Allocation Rule score over time and a change in share of wallet was nominally the largest overall.[13] The findings of this investigation were published in the *Journal of Service Management,* a peer-reviewed academic journal in the field of service management.[14]

Other researchers have also investigated the Wallet Allocation Rule and found similar results. In one of the most comprehensive investigations, researchers Alice Louw and Jan Hofmeyr compared correlations between the Wallet Allocation Rule and two more complex approaches with customers' actual share of category spending in three industries.[15] Although the survey questions used were not the same across the three approaches investigated, the findings were. The Wallet Allocation Rule worked as well as these more complex approaches.[16]

Most new approaches rely on anecdotes to support their claims (e.g., "Firm X adopted this new approach, and it transformed its business"). Although it is always nice to have a story, anecdotes mean something only if they are proved to work across companies and industries.

As these different investigations make clear, the Wallet Allocation Rule has undergone numerous, rigorous scientific tests. More important, it has passed them all!

The "Best" Metric?

The Wallet Allocation Rule makes it possible for managers to easily link their customer metrics to share of wallet. But in a world of many competing metrics (satisfaction, NPS, etc.) what is the *best* metric to track?

In recent years, researchers have advanced a number of customer metrics purported to be the best at linking customer survey data to business outcomes. But the best metrics have shown only modest correlations to growth. None have shown themselves to be universally effective across all competitive environments. And all of these metrics have proved to be weak predictors of share of wallet. Nevertheless, the weaknesses of existing metrics have not discouraged managers from adopting new ones in hopes of gaining better insight into customer behavior.

In picking a best metric, it is important to recognize that the most commonly used metrics are highly correlated with one another. In fact, statistical analysis of these metrics reveals that they are actually measuring the same construct. So although it is possible that one metric

Satisfaction

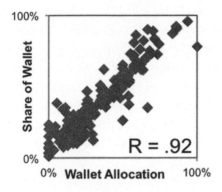

Purchase Intention

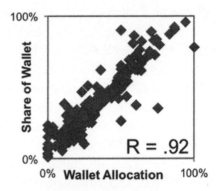

Recommend Intention

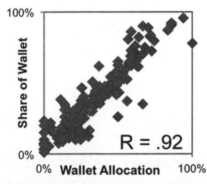

Net Promoter Score
Recommend intention using NPS classifications

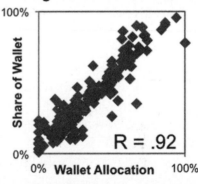

FIGURE 2.5 It Doesn't Matter Which Metric You Use When Using the Wallet Allocation Rule

Surprisingly, performance was virtually identical regardless of the metric used to determine a firm's/brand's relative performance ranking. Note: Scatter diagrams show the average share of wallet at the firm/brand level (*y*-axis) by the predicted average share of wallet using the Wallet Allocation Rule (*x*-axis).

would perform somewhat better than another in some situations, the likelihood that any one metric would be an obvious winner seems highly unlikely.

A key implication of the Wallet Allocation Rule is that the primary problem in linking these measures to share of wallet is in the use of absolute scores, not in the choice of metric. To determine whether this was indeed the case, we examined the linkage of the most commonly used satisfaction/loyalty metrics to share of wallet when using the Wallet Allocation Rule.

Although we expected all metrics to perform reasonably well when using the Wallet Allocation Rule, we did not expect the almost identical results we found (see Figure 2.5). Our findings indicate that efforts to uncover the best metric are misplaced. Certainly, there will be isolated cases in which one metric outperforms another. However, it appears that managers in most industries do not need to switch the customer metrics (satisfaction, NPS, etc.) that they have been tracking over time if they wish to have a strong linkage to share of wallet. Rather, they simply need to apply the Wallet Allocation Rule.

Why Does the Wallet Allocation Rule Work?

It is intuitive that the amount a customer spends on a brand would be a function of how that person ranked that brand vis-à-vis other competitors also used. We would naturally expect the preferred choice to be used more than the next best choice.

But the foundation of the Wallet Allocation Rule goes beyond intuition. The crux of the rule states that share of wallet is a function of a brand's rank. This relationship reflects a scientific empirical law, referred to as Zipf's law.[17]

In the 1930s, Harvard linguist George Kingsley Zipf discovered that the frequency of any word in a language is inversely proportional to its rank. Since then, scientists have found similar relationships for a wide variety of situations, including Internet usage, world income distribution, population ranks of cities, the size and frequency of earthquakes, and note usage in musical compositions.

Most important for managers, academic researchers have known for some time that the market shares of companies follow this law. As a result, the most widely proposed alternatives to the Wallet Allocation Rule to link to share of wallet use the Zipf distribution (a mathematical formula based on Zipf's law).

Although Zipf's law is conceptually simple, most managers would find it difficult to calculate the Zipf distribution. Mathematically, the formula for calculating share of wallet using the Zipf distribution is as follows:

$$Share \; of \; wallet = \cfrac{1}{rank_{ij}^{s(m_i)} \left[\sum_{k=1}^{m_i} \left(\cfrac{1}{rank_{ik}^{s(m_i)}} \right) \right]}$$

where $s(m_i)$ is a constant that depends on the number of brands (m_i).

Finding the optimal Zipf distribution requires inputting both rank and share of wallet data into a software application and then computationally back-solving to determine the appropriate values of s in the preceding equation.

This is clearly complicated. Worse still, the model is difficult to convey to senior managers and to the organization at large. The reality is that managers tend to reject overly complicated models because they intuitively don't understand them, can't communicate them, and certainly can't rally the organization around them. As a result, they "revert to models of great simplicity."[18]

Unfortunately, the ultrasimple models (e.g., absolute satisfaction and NPS) do not link to the share of spending that customers give to the brands they use. They may be simple, but no manager will knowingly accept wrong. And if the goal is to drive share of wallet, they are most definitely the wrong metrics to use.

With the Wallet Allocation Rule, managers can easily link their customer metrics to share of wallet without requiring a PhD in statistics. All you need to know is the number of brands that customers use and their rank.

Using the Wallet Allocation Rule

Although the Wallet Allocation Rule isn't as simple as calculating your firm's NPS, it isn't difficult either. To quote the *Harvard Business Review,* "Don't let the math scare you."[19] Using the Wallet Allocation Rule is a very simple three-step process.

Step 1: Survey customers to determine the brands (or stores or firms) they regularly use in the product category you want to analyze. Let's say that John, Jane, Mary, and Tom all use the same brands of detergent: Brands X, Y, and Z.

Step 2: Gauge satisfaction (or another common loyalty metric, such as NPS) for each brand the customer uses; then convert those scores into ranks. The highest-scoring brand for a customer would be ranked first, the second-highest second, and so forth.

Figure 2.6 shows the satisfaction ratings for three brands of detergent for John, Jane, Mary, and Tom.

Figure 2.7 shows the ranks of the three detergents based on the satisfaction scores provided by John, Jane, Mary, and Tom.

In the case of a tie, as was the case for Tom with Brand Y and Brand Z, assign each brand a rank using the average of the two spots they would have occupied had they not been tied.

Brands not used are treated as missing and are not assigned a rank, as was the case for Jane with Brand Y.

Step 3: To arrive at a brand's share of wallet for a given customer, plug the brand's rank and the number of brands used by the customer into the Wallet Allocation Rule formula:

$$\text{Share of wallet} = \left(1 - \frac{rank}{number\ of\ brands + 1}\right)$$
$$\times \left(\frac{2}{number\ of\ brands}\right)$$

For example, John's share for Brand Z is as follows:

$$= \left(1 - \frac{1}{3+1}\right) \times \left(\frac{2}{3}\right)$$
$$= (1 - 0.25) \times (0.666667)$$
$$= 50 \text{ percent}$$

	Brand X	Brand Y	Brand Z
JOHN	8	9	10
JANE	7	not used	9
MARY	6	9	8
TOM	7	9	9

FIGURE 2.6 Customers' Satisfaction Levels with Brands X, Y, and Z

	Brand X	Brand Y	Brand Z
JOHN	3	2	1
JANE	2	--	1
MARY	3	1	2
TOM	3	1.5	1.5

FIGURE 2.7 Customers' Relative "Ranked" Satisfaction Levels with Brands X, Y, and Z

	Brand X	Brand Y	Brand Z
JOHN	16.7%	33.3%	50.0%
JANE	33.3%	0%	66.7%
MARY	16.7%	50.0%	33.3%
TOM	16.7%	41.7%	41.7%
BRAND SHARE OF WALLET (ALL CUSTOMERS)	20.9%	31.3%	47.9%
BRAND SHARE OF WALLET (BRAND USERS ONLY)	20.9%	41.7%	47.9%

FIGURE 2.8 Brand-Level Share of Wallet

Repeat the calculation for each customer and brand. To obtain the average share of wallet your customers give to a particular brand, simply average individual customers' share-of-wallet scores. There are two ways to do this (see Figure 2.8).

- *All customers:* This is the average share of wallet going to a brand from all of your customers. This provides a quick look at the overall financial opportunity represented by a specific competitor.

- *Brand users only:* This is the average share of wallet going to a brand from your customers who use this brand (i.e., noncustomers of the brand are excluded). This provides insight into the strength of the relationship that your customers who use a competing brand feel toward that brand.

Wallet Allocation Rule Strategy

Several important strategic issues stem directly from the Wallet Allocation Rule.

- *Strategic issue 1:* First and foremost, managers cannot evaluate their firms without taking competition into account. Although this sounds obvious, the reality is that managers typically evaluate their performance using customer perceptions of their firm only. As a result, the target objectives used to evaluate and compensate managers are almost never based on changing the perceived rank of the firm vis-à-vis competition. Rather, they are based on achieving a particular score for the firm.

- *Strategic issue 2:* Rank matters! Every manager knows that it is better to be number one than number two. But the Wallet Allocation Rule makes it very easy for managers to determine the financial implications of that. The difference between first and second is typically quite large (see Figure 2.9). And making that jump can have a tremendous financial impact.

- *Strategic issue 3:* Parity hurts! The Wallet Allocation Rule also makes clear that it is not enough for your brand to be tied for first place. There must be a reason for customers to prefer your firm. Otherwise, you evenly divide your customers' share of wallet with your closest competitors (see Figure 2.10).

- *Strategic issue 4:* The more brands a customer uses, the lower the potential for everyone. The number of competitors that your customers use has a significant impact on customers' share of wallet (see Figure 2.11). Ranking first in a field of three is much better

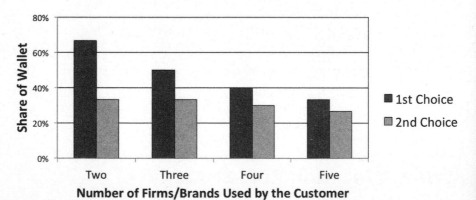

FIGURE 2.9 The Difference between First Choice and Second Choice Is Typically Quite Large

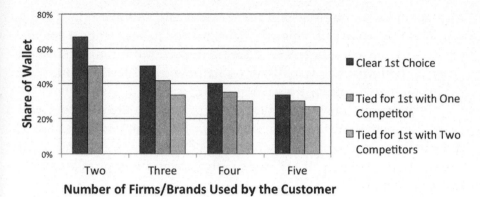

FIGURE 2.10 Parity Hurts

There must be a reason for customers to prefer your firm to its strongest competitors. Otherwise, customers evenly divide their share of wallet with your brand and its closest competitors.

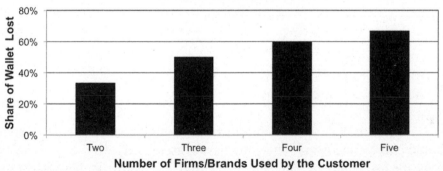

FIGURE 2.11 The More Brands Used by a Customer, the Lower the Potential Share of Everyone

Reducing the number of brands a customer uses dramatically increases the share of wallet for the first choice brand. Therefore, when possible, managers need to incorporate differentiating aspects of lower-ranked brands into their firm's offer to reduce customers' usage of the competitor.

than ranking first in a field of six. That's because every brand used by a customer gets some percentage of his or her wallet.

These strategic issues have practical implications for how we identify opportunities for improving share of wallet. The traditional approach to pinpointing opportunities involves answering the question, "What can we do to make you happier?" Whether you're analyzing customers' open-ended survey responses or deriving importance through statistical analysis, the focus is almost always on improving satisfaction with what the firm or brand currently offers.

Performance, however, is relative to competitive alternatives. Obviously, improving satisfaction is important. This is primarily because at some point, increases in satisfaction make a brand more attractive to customers relative to competitors. But simply striving for improved satisfaction is not enough.

Managers also need to understand exactly why customers use each of the brands that they do. Customers have legitimate reasons for using multiple brands in a category. Therefore, efforts designed to improve share of wallet that do not address precisely why *your* customers also use your competitors are doomed.

Managers can gather this information as part of the Wallet Allocation Rule survey process. And this process doesn't have to be complex. It can be as simple as asking customers something like the following:

> *When choosing between brands, what tends to be the deciding factor in choosing one over the other?*
> *I choose [Brand 1] when …*
> *I choose [Brand 2] when …*

Armed with an understanding of why your customers use both your brand and competitive brands, managers can identify what it really takes to be the first choice of their customers. And because the Wallet Allocation Rule is tied to share of wallet, managers can prioritize their efforts by their potential impact on future revenues.

How to Improve Your Rank

One of the key takeaways of the Wallet Allocation Rule is that if you want to improve your share, you need to improve your rank. Improving rank, however, is not the same as improving your overall satisfaction or NPS level. Improving your rank requires minimizing the reasons customers feel the need to use the competition.

Following is an easy-to-follow process you can implement right away to improve your share:

1. Survey a statistically valid sample of your customers to find out how they rank you and the competitors they also purchase from.
2. Apply the Wallet Allocation Rule to establish the share of wallet of each competitor.
3. Determine how many of your customers use each competitor.
4. Calculate the revenue that goes from your customers to each competitor.
5. Identify the primary reasons your customers use your competitors.
6. Prioritize your opportunities to improve your share of wallet: Estimate the cost of addressing each reason your customers choose a competitor and weigh those costs against your potential financial return in each case. Remember to take into account the cumulative impact of addressing issues that apply to multiple competitors.

The Rule in Practice

To see how this would work in the real world, let's look at a case drawn from our research. Management at a grocery retail chain surveys its customers and finds that most customers are happy with their experience; 53 percent of customers would be classified as promoters using the NPS classification system (in the "would recommend" category, they rate the store a 9 or 10 on a scale of 0 to 10).

Despite these good scores, however, only 43 percent of customers would classify the grocer as their first choice. In other words, 57 percent either prefer one or more of the grocer's competitors or consider the grocer to be at parity with them.

To understand the financial implications, the grocer used the Wallet Allocation Rule to calculate how much of its customers' spending is going to its competitors. To do this, the grocer first calculated the average share of wallet it gets from its customers and the portion its competitors get from its customers.

Next, because share of wallet reflects the percentage of spending customers give to a brand, the grocer multiplied share of wallet estimates by its customers' average monthly grocery spend and the number of its customers who also patronize the competing stores. The results indicated that its top three competitors were extracting $425 million from its customers' wallets.

To understand what could be done to get some of this money back, the grocer analyzed its survey data to understand what was driving customers' spending behaviors.

The company conducted an analysis to determine the most important drivers of its NPS. This analysis revealed that the top two reasons customers recommend the grocer are the quality of its produce and the ambience of the store. This was no surprise to management, as the grocer competes by positioning itself on providing superior produce and maintaining a quality store atmosphere.

An analysis of the drivers of rank, however, showed that improving these attributes would not result in customers giving the grocer a greater share of their spending on groceries. The analysis revealed that the grocer's customers are using the competition for completely different reasons.

For one competitor, the primary attraction is everyday low prices. Another competitor also competes on price, but largely through rotating deep discounts. And a third competitor's main appeal is the convenience of its locations—it had large numbers of smaller stores distributed throughout metropolitan areas.

For the grocer to move up to first place in more of its customers' minds, it can't simply do more of what it already does well; providing even better produce or enhancing the aesthetics might further delight customers who already rank it first but would be unlikely to change the minds of the rest, who are mainly interested in low prices and convenience.

The analysis made clear that, at least in the short term, focusing on the convenience-based competitor was not a realistic option. The grocer certainly wasn't going to be able to open lots of new stores to have comparable levels of convenience.

This meant that the grocer was forced to focus on its price-based competitors if it wanted to get a greater share of its customers' wallets. Of course, a high-quality ambience, high-quality produce store is never going to be the price leader—its costs of operations are naturally higher.

Matching price, however, is not the goal. The goal is to reduce customers' need to use the competition.

To do this, the grocer determined what customers were actually buying from the competition. Because the company had good information on the purchases its customers made, it could easily see what its customers were purchasing. More important, it could see what they were not purchasing but would be expected to purchase as part of a total grocery shopping basket. It also confirmed the items that were going to competitors through customer surveys.

These missed purchases tended to be staple goods, such as bread, milk, sugar, and flour. Because staples tend to offer little differentiation, they largely compete on price. So the fact that many of the grocer's customers choose to purchase staples from the cheaper competitors resonated with management.

This also presented management with a problem. There was no way that the grocer could profitably match the lowest price on most staples.

Instead, the grocer reasoned that it should take advantage of the fact that its customers are already attracted to the store for its produce and ambience. Because customers are already visiting the grocer, management's goal should be to make it less economically attractive for customers to shop multiple grocery stores. This, however, doesn't require being the price leader. Instead of matching the cheapest competitor, the grocer lowered the price on its most commonly purchased staples to a relevant level—low enough that more customers perceived it was better to consolidate their grocery purchases into one shopping trip.

Surveys after the price change found that 49 percent of customers considered the grocer their first choice (a gain of 6 percent). Moreover, the average number of stores customers regularly shopped dropped from 2.5 to 2.0. These changes, when plugged into the Wallet Allocation Rule, translate to a 7-point increase in share of wallet—the equivalent of shifting $62 million from competitors' registers into the grocer's own.

Conclusion

Many companies could see this kind of revenue jump if they decided to stop pursuing customer satisfaction for its own sake and instead focused on how satisfaction and other loyalty boosters could help them pull ahead of the competition.

The Wallet Allocation Rule turns traditional satisfaction measurement on its head. The rule shifts the emphasis from internally focused satisfaction measurement to your brand's competitive position in the marketplace.

Brands exist in the market, not in a vacuum, and that's the way to approach performance. Sounds elementary, right? Yet most managers treat satisfaction and loyalty metrics as if just achieving a particular score is sufficient. The reality is that simply boosting your brand's satisfaction ratings rarely increases your share of wallet—but improving your brand's rank does.

The Wallet Allocation Rule allows you to build strategies that directly affect brand performance and then measure their impact on share of wallet.

What do managers normally do to try to improve share of wallet? Typically, they create programs and initiatives designed to improve customer happiness and then measure success based on satisfaction. Increased customer happiness is important, but it rarely has the desired effect on the bottom line.

Managers should instead focus their energy on understanding why their consumers use the brands they do. If your brand is not their top choice, find out why they prefer your competitor's brand over yours.

By applying the Wallet Allocation Rule, managers get real insight into the money they currently get from their customers, the money available to be earned from them, and what it takes to get it.

If growing your share is what you're after, you won't learn much from watching changes in your satisfaction scores. Focus instead on how to pull ahead of your competition. That's what makes a champion.

The Wallet Allocation Rule in Action

The more original a discovery, the more obvious it seems afterwards.[1]

—*Arthur Koestler, author and journalist*

Linda Wolf, former chair and chief executive officer (CEO) of Leo Burnett Worldwide observed, "Before you can have a share of market, you must have a share of mind."[2] This mind-set drives most companies' marketing budgets. Companies spend hundreds of billions of dollars each year to capture share of customers' minds. In fact, AT&T and Verizon—the two biggest advertisers in the United States—spent $3 billion (approximately $1.5 billion each) in 2013 to attract customers to their brands.[3]

This chapter benefited greatly from the insight and writing of numerous Ipsos Loyalty colleagues from around the world. Each of these contributors is recognized as principal contributors in the Acknowledgments section at the end of this book.

Of course, the reason for this massive spending is that getting customers to seriously consider using a brand is no easy task. For customers to change their regular buying behaviors, they first must think about why they should. Given the numerous purchases that each of us makes every week, it is completely unrealistic to expect this for most of the things we buy. We would never make it out of the grocery store if we seriously considered the alternatives for everything we put in our shopping carts.

As purchase decisions become routine for most brands, appealing to customers requires a winning strategy. Inside the walls of every company are groups of people trying to figure out how to attract new customers and keep their current customers and also get them to buy more. The anemic growth rates of most companies, however, demonstrate just how hard that is to do.

Grinding a New Set of Lenses

The aim of any strategy is to gain an advantage over competitors, but strategic advantage can be fluid. The history of modern management has shown that competitive advantage can be built slowly over time or captured in a moment as market newcomers leapfrog traditional players.

There are many paths to successful strategy and marketplace differentiation. The one constant is that customers must view the outcome of that strategy as being in their interest if it is going to be successful.

One of the most high-profile examples of failing to convince customers that a company's new strategy is in their best interest is the saga of JCPenney, later rebranded JCP. CEO Ron Johnson inherited an older brand that played competitively in a distinct way: having the right sizes, decent pricing with the option to "stack" coupons, and an everyday feel to the brands it provided. Johnson changed everything about the firm: the brands, the pricing strategy, the brand image, and the store layout.

One of the most disconcerting changes for customers, however, was a switch to "everyday fair pricing." This meant customers could no longer enjoy the fun of coupon stacking and shopping for that perfect $50 shirt for 90 percent off.

Interestingly, Johnson's pricing plan lowered customers' overall annual spending on average. Still, customers defected in droves, leading to continuous sales losses and store closings. As a result, Johnson's fate was sealed and the former CEO was restored, bringing with him an apology tour and the return of traditional brands and pricing—and customers began to return.

As the JCPenney story demonstrates, the best-laid plans either win or lose in the hearts, minds, and wallets of customers. Therefore, the first step in a winning strategy is to actually think like your customers. This requires seeing the world as they see it.

Although this sounds easy, it most definitely is not. Managers think about their brands constantly. For most brands, however, customers think about them only when they are compelled to think about them. Moreover, when customers do think about your brand, they think about it relative to whatever else they could be doing with their time or money.

The simple rule that managers must never forget is this: No customer knowingly spends his or her money to have an inferior experience. They either believe that this is the best choice for their hard-earned money, or they go elsewhere.

Of course, this is (or should be) obvious. The strange thing is that it is not reflected in how companies typically measure, analyze, or manage the customer experience. What is required is a fundamental shift in how managers view their customer data.

Managers treat their customer metrics as if they existed in a vacuum. Sure, they might benchmark key competitors, but the measures that they actually use to drive and reward improvement are almost always inward looking. For example, companies frequently set target customer satisfaction or Net Promoter Score (NPS) levels for employee bonuses. By contrast, rarely do companies set performance thresholds for being customers' preferred brand in the category.

The Wallet Allocation Rule requires that managers take a customer-centric perspective. It forces managers to consider the rank that each customer assigns to their brands vis-à-vis the competition. In the end, it is all about giving customers fewer reasons to use the competition.

Putting the Wallet Allocation Rule to Work

The scientific evidence that the Wallet Allocation Rule works across cultures and industries is indisputable.[4] Most managers, however, are not scientific researchers. As a result, they often are uncomfortable relying on scientific evidence alone. Moreover, scientific research frequently suffers from the problem of dullness combined with mind-numbing statistics. Still, it is the only way to prove that something really works.

The good news is that most managers are willing to accept that the Wallet Allocation Rule strongly links to share of wallet. And it is very easy to prove that the metrics companies are currently using do not.

What is less obvious to managers, however, is how using the Wallet Allocation Rule approach leads to different conclusions. If, in the end, you get the same answer regarding what to do, then why go through the pain of change?

Managers using the Wallet Allocation Rule system do not get the same answers. This is because Wallet Allocation Rule analysis revolves around understanding the key drivers of a brand's relative rank vis-à-vis competition, not the traditional drivers of satisfaction or NPS. It also requires that managers recognize the market barriers that affect customers' ability to buy a preferred brand. (Key driver analysis and market barriers are discussed in more detail in Chapter 5.) When viewing markets from this perspective, it becomes clear what is really driving customers' decisions about where to spend their money.

What follows are examples of Wallet Allocation Rule thinking across different countries and industries. Each case briefly captures the essence of viewing a company and its competitive position using a Wallet Allocation Rule framework. They are designed to be self-contained so that readers can pick and choose those cases most relevant to them.

Credit Unions in the United States

Credit unions serve more than 90 million members in the United States.[5] Credit unions differ from other financial institutions in that they are nonprofit, member-owned companies. In general, however, U.S. credit unions offer most of the same core services as their retail banking competitors (e.g., checking, savings, CDs—although they may use different names for these services).

Credit unions typically have much higher satisfaction and NPS levels than their banking competitors. In fact, they have achieved record-high satisfaction levels when compared with all other industries in the United States.[6] Despite this, credit unions hold less than 10 percent of U.S. deposits.[7]

To understand the factors that drive credit union members to use multiple financial institutions, in 2012 we conducted a study with 4,712 credit union depositors.[8] The results revealed that more than 65 percent of credit union depositors use one or more competing financial institutions.

As expected, satisfaction and NPS levels were much higher for credit unions than for their bank competitors. Satisfaction and NPS, however, explained only 9 percent of the variation in customers' share of deposits (see Figure 3.1). By contrast, the Wallet Allocation Rule explained 55 percent of variance in members' share of deposit allocations, and 90 percent of the variance at the credit union/bank level (see Figure 3.2).

Next we conducted a key driver analysis similar to what most financial institutions currently use to uncover the factors that most influenced satisfaction. We also conducted a Wallet Allocation Rule key driver analysis to uncover the factors that most affected how members ranked the various financial institutions they used.

The analysis revealed that the top driver of satisfaction with credit unions was the company's resolution of customer complaints. Of course, this makes complete sense. Issues worthy of complaining clearly lower satisfaction, so fixing problems is bound to have a positive impact on customers' overall satisfaction levels.

But if you really think about it, pouring resources into complaint resolution may not improve a credit union's share of deposits. How many customers actually select a credit union because it is good at resolving their complaints? This probably wasn't a major reason for most customers.

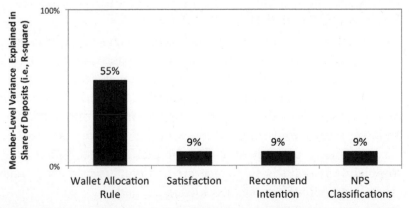

FIGURE 3.1 The Relationship of Various Metrics to Members' Share of Deposits

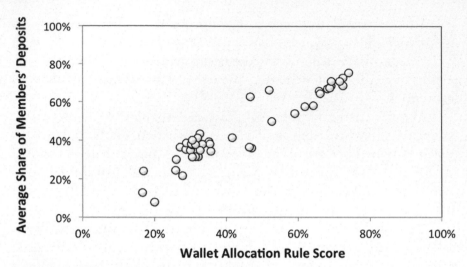

FIGURE 3.2 The Relationship between the Wallet Allocation Rule and Share of Wallet (at the Financial Institution Level)

By contrast, the research uncovered that the most important driver of rank (and ultimately share of deposits) was the competitiveness of fees. Low fees are a strong feature of credit unions when compared with banks (see Figure 3.3).

Despite lower fees, better complaint resolution, and considerably higher overall satisfaction (and NPS) levels, however, the majority of credit union customers also felt the need to use one or more competing financial institutions. A separate analysis reveals why. The most important driver of a competing bank's share among credit union members was Internet banking services. Internet banking is a strong feature of banks compared with credit unions (see Figure 3.4).

This example highlights the need for understanding drivers beyond traditional satisfaction frameworks. The natural takeaway from the traditional analysis of satisfaction is that credit unions need to focus on the in—credit union experience (i.e., complaint resolution). This finding is almost certainly true in the sense that failure on this dimension would lead to lower satisfaction scores, which would ultimately affect the credit union's rank among its competitors. Yet this picture is incomplete. Reducing complaints is unlikely to reduce credit union customers' perceived need to use competing financial institutions.

Even understanding the top driver of rank for credit union customers may offer an incomplete understanding of opportunities for growth.

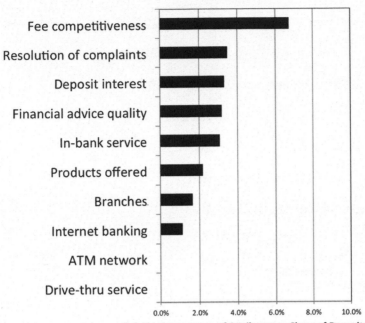

FIGURE 3.3 Drivers of Share of Deposits for Credit Unions

In this case, competitiveness of fees is the top driver of rank for credit unions. So leveraging this advantage further, either through changes in fee structure or emphasis in communication, could increase a credit union's share of deposits.

Credit unions, however, already have much lower fees than banks. In fact, fees are frequently nonexistent. As a result, there is little opportunity for credit unions to reduce fees further—unless they want to pay customers to use their services. The point here is that growth cannot be achieved by credit unions simply doing better on the things that they already do well.

It is only when you look at the drivers of competitors' share within your own customer base that areas of greatest opportunity present themselves. Your customers use other brands for a reason. Commercial banks filled a need for Internet-based banking that credit unions did not meet. This shows that the greatest share can be gained by eliminating your customers' need to use competitors.

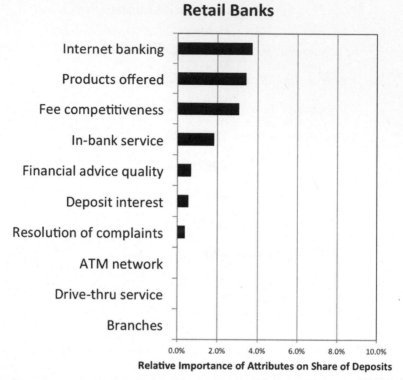

FIGURE 3.4 Drivers of Share of Deposits for Retail Banks by Credit Union Members

So although few industries can approach the level of satisfaction of credit unions, gaining share of deposits requires mitigating banks' advantages in areas important to credit union members. Fortunately, this is doable. And the financial rewards for doing so are worth the effort. Our research finds that for credit union depositors who use more than one financial institution, $25,414 in deposits on average is going to competing institutions.

Quick-Serve Restaurants in Canada

The Canadian quick-serve restaurant (QSR) market is similar to many Western QSR markets: highly competitive with many national chains vying for share along with smaller local outlets. Because of the wide variety of choices, leveraging the important contributors to share of wallet is imperative to business growth.

Many QSR chains deploy NPS or satisfaction-based customer measurement programs that are designed to catalog customer experiences while those memories are fresh. Survey invitations have grown to be ubiquitous mainstays on customer receipts; notices on the receipts point patrons to a website or a phone number. These surveys invariably ask for ratings of performance on food quality, service speed, accessibility, customer service, and employee courtesy and other similar attributes.

These surveys are routinely analyzed to improve both individual location improvements—issues affecting a specific location (e.g., "This location is not always clean, and there's never any parking")—as well as corporate structural improvements that could affect the firm nationwide (e.g., "No matter where I go, your egg sandwiches are never very good").

These programs can even zero-in on customers who have painfully bad experiences, calling back low-rated customers to see if the relationship can be restored. There are many colloquial stories about bad in-store experiences where an angry customer is converted to a customer for life when the chief customer officer contacts him to apologize for bad service and offers a small-dollar coupon for a free meal.

Often, results from these programs are relayed back to every store manager for direct, tactical action (e.g., calling back the customer), or broader action (e.g., improving cleanliness at a particular outlet). These programs are invaluable for operational management to focus actions and improve performance in a measurable way.

The flaw in these programs is that the rating system simply does not accurately portend future customer behavior or alert head office management to the factors that are driving share of spend in the marketplace. Therefore, to understand whether or not there is a significant return on their improvement investments, QSRs need to accompany this transactional research with an additional layer that ensures their research is both tactical and strategic.

In an independent 2014 benchmarking study of five national-chain quick serve restaurants, the flaw in using a satisfaction-only measurement approach is clearly revealed.

To demonstrate this point, we conceal the brand names and allow you to focus only on the numbers. Figure 3.5 shows Top-2 box satisfaction scores (a satisfaction rating of 9 or 10 on a 10-point scale) for each brand, which reveals particular areas of strength and weakness.

	Customer Service	Convenience	Menu Range	Pleasing Environment	Accessibility (Parking and Drive-Thru)	Speed
Brand 1	42%	37%	48%	42%	39%	39%
Brand 2	28%	39%	29%	28%	33%	31%
Brand 3	41%	51%	31%	41%	34%	35%
Brand 4	27%	14%	5%	36%	4%	9%
Brand 5	42%	57%	45%	45%	36%	52%

FIGURE 3.5 Top-2 Box Satisfaction Levels

Using satisfaction data alone might lead Brand 4 to conclude that it needs to improve its *menu range* and *accessibility*. Similarly, Brand 5 might conclude that it has an advantage on *convenience* and *speed* and that, with minor improvements, it could become the leader on *accessibility*.

Traditional key driver analysis outlines the contribution of each of these attributes in explaining customer satisfaction. The higher an impact score, the more important it is in creating customer delight.

Using this traditional analysis, Brand 1 and Brand 5 would conclude that *menu range* is their most important area of focus; Brand 3 would conclude that it needs to allocate energy equally between *environment, convenience,* and *customer service* but less on *speed, accessibility,* and *menu range*.

The problem at the outset is that the correlation between satisfaction and share of wallet (i.e., actual business results) is very low. Clearly, a large component of consumer choice is based on factors other than satisfaction, so using satisfaction data to guide performance improvements will lead to higher satisfaction, no doubt, but not necessarily better financial results.

Using Brand 3 as our example, *environment, convenience,* and *customer service* are the key drivers of satisfaction. When using the Wallet Allocation Rule approach to understand the drivers of share of wallet, however, a dramatically different picture emerges altogether. The keys to financial success are *convenience, customer service, speed,* and *accessibility* (see Figure 3.6).

This makes complete sense when we reveal that Brand 3 is Tim Hortons. For those unaware, Tim Hortons is a ubiquitous fast-service food and coffee chain with 3,588 locations in Canada and is Canada's largest food service operator. To put this in perspective, there is one Tim Hortons

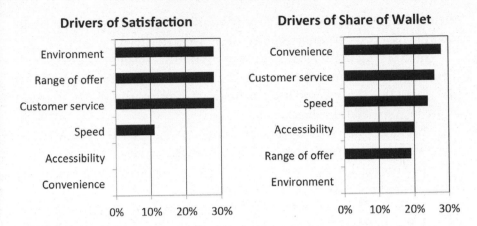

FIGURE 3.6 Drivers of Satisfaction and Share of Wallet for Tim Hortons

location for approximately every 9,700 Canadians. Compare this with one Dunkin' Donuts for approximately every 44,700 Americans, or one Costa Coffee for every 53,800 Britons.

Although known for its coffee and doughnuts, choosing Tim Hortons is often based as much on its convenience and distribution strength as it is the quality of its fare.

Similar to Tim Hortons, all brands experience gaps between what makes customers happy and what keeps them coming back. Certainly in the case of Tim Hortons, a weaker customer service experience could drive overall satisfaction down—losing a competitive ranking position—and force customers to consider alternatives.

In the end, however, driving satisfaction tells only part of the story, and understanding what drives share of wallet ensures that the right measures are making it to the corporate scorecard.

Retail Banking in the United Kingdom

The retail banking market in the United Kingdom, as in many other developed markets globally is characterized by the fact that consumers typically have relationships with multiple providers. Despite this high level of multibanking, however, banking relationships tend to be typified by a high level of inertia. Only 2.8 percent of UK retail banking customers switched their checking accounts (called "current accounts" in the UK) in 2012.

To understand what underpins this inertia, as well as the push-and-pull factors that influence those who do change their banking relationships, we can apply Wallet Allocation Rule analysis to ascertain the influences on customers' choice of provider.

In 2012, we conducted a study among British bank customers with the goal of understanding more about their relationships with providers. The aim of this study was to investigate the stability of the relative position of the major brands in the category.

The largest brand in the market at the time was Lloyds TSB, although it has subsequently been split into two brands as a result of a European Commission legal ruling following UK government intervention in the banking market in 2008; more about this later.

At the time of our research, 44 percent of Lloyds TSB customers named the brand as their sole banking provider. This meant that the remaining majority (56 percent) had multiple checking account relationships with different institutions. Of those having multiple relationships, only a minority (13 percent of all customers) said that they rated Lloyds TSB higher in terms of overall satisfaction than their other providers. Despite its market-leading position, this indicated that Lloyds TSB could not take any of its customer relationships for granted.

Of the 56 percent who have more than a single checking account, more than three out of four rated Lloyds as on-par with competitors or worse. Despite its incredible heritage and market position, losses on possible customer revenue were apparent.

The competitiveness of the market was further evidenced by the proportion of customers who had relationships with competitors of Lloyds TSB, which highlighted the competitive challenge in the marketplace (see Figure 3.7).

Given the relatively high likelihood of customers with multiple banking relationships to rate competitive brands at least as good as Lloyds TSB (and in many cases better), Wallet Allocation Rule analysis indicated that the most effective method for improving financial results was to identify performance improvements that would encourage a graduation in satisfaction ranking.

To facilitate this, we used Wallet Allocation Rule key driver analysis to identify the following:

1. The areas that have the highest impact on Lloyds TSB customers' share of wallet (defined as the point at which increasing the mean score on an attribute would improve Lloyds TSB's rank compared with competitors)

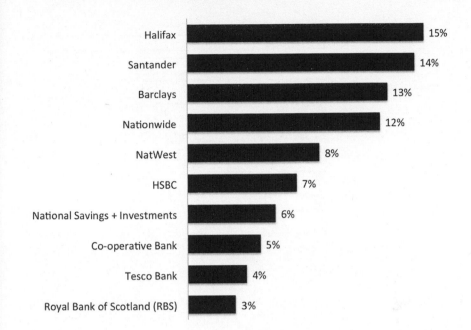

FIGURE 3.7 Other Banks Used as a Percent of Total Lloyds TSB Customers

2. The areas that have the highest impact on Lloyds TSB retaining its customers (defined as the point at which increasing the mean score would have an impact but would not improve the bank's rank)

Figure 3.8 shows the relative impact of improving performance for a particular attribute on an individual's rating of Lloyds TSB compared with its competitors. These data are broken down by the impact on share of wallet and retention.

Across all of the drivers shown in Figure 3.8, the branch network had the greatest overall impact on Lloyds TSB's satisfaction ranking, and this is particularly important for retaining customers. At the time, Lloyds TSB had the most extensive network of branches, and the ability to access a local branch was a key factor influencing its ability to retain customers. This is especially notable because—unlike the United States and many other world markets—UK banks do not charge automated teller machine (ATM) fees for noncustomers. The result is that the impact of ATM networks is low, further highlighting the role of the branch staff and services as core to servicing Lloyd's relationships.

Subsequent events, however, conspired to erode this key competitive advantage. In 2008 the EU Commission forced Lloyds TSB to

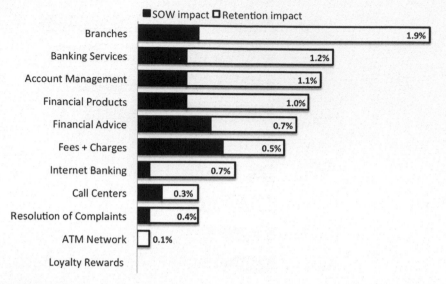

FIGURE 3.8 Lloyds TSB Branches Are Important for Retention and Share of Wallet, but Improving Fees + Charges and Financial Advice Offer the Greatest Opportunity to Increase Share of Wallet

split, resulting in a reduction of 631 branches, 5 million customers, 8 million accounts, and 8,000 staff. In September 2013, Lloyds TSB was separated into Lloyds Bank and TSB, which reduced the Lloyds Bank branch network by 32 percent.

Until this point, Lloyds TSB had benefited the most in terms of customers' perceptions of the effort required to move accounts and, when quantified, the relative importance of this "barrier to switching" cannot be underestimated (see Figure 3.9).

Just when the greatest barrier to switching providers was taken away, the second greatest barrier to switching (the convenience of branch location) was similarly eradicated for many customers with the separation of Lloyds and TSB.

To encourage competitiveness in the UK personal checking account market and help overcome the evident inertia among consumers, in September 2013, the UK Payments Council—an organization of financial institutions in the UK that sets strategy for evolution in payment mechanisms—launched a new "switching service" backed by the Current Account Switch Guarantee, designed "to let you switch your current account from one bank or building society to another in a simple, reliable and hassle-free way." [9]

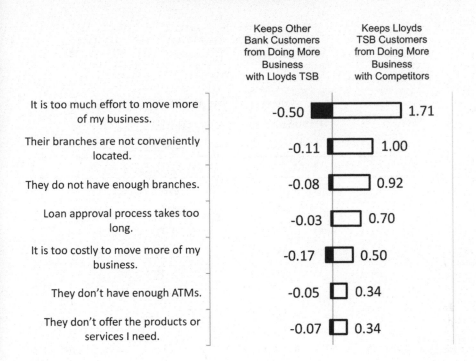

	Keeps Other Bank Customers from Doing More Business with Lloyds TSB	Keeps Lloyds TSB Customers from Doing More Business with Competitors
It is too much effort to move more of my business.	-0.50	1.71
Their branches are not conveniently located.	-0.11	1.00
They do not have enough branches.	-0.08	0.92
Loan approval process takes too long.	-0.03	0.70
It is too costly to move more of my business.	-0.17	0.50
They don't have enough ATMs.	-0.05	0.34
They don't offer the products or services I need.	-0.07	0.34

FIGURE 3.9 The Impact of Negative and Positive Barriers for Lloyds TSB

Like the establishment of cell phone number portability in the United States, which freed individuals of a tether to a single carrier, this process removed a structural barrier that worked in favor of the most capital-dominant institutions.

The Current Account Switch Guarantee ultimately reduced a switching process that previously could have taken up to six weeks down to one week. Although overall checking account switching levels remained relatively low, checking account switching volumes from January to June 2013 were up 16 percent in the same six-month period in 2014, possibly indicating that as the market calmed down, portable relationships could influence future growth intentions.

Timed well to coincide with this developing market opportunity, Santander launched an added-value checking account product in the UK—the 123 Current Account—which activated a significant "pull" factor and encouraged switching among banking customers. By July 2014, more than 200,000 current account holders had switched to Santander.

Our 2012 analysis of potential challengers for Lloyds TSB identified Santander as one of the greatest challengers to Lloyds TSB's

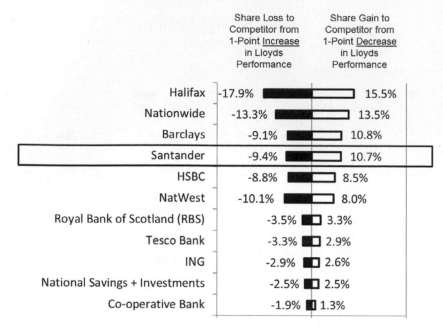

FIGURE 3.10 Potential Market Impact on Competitors from a Change in Lloyds TSB Performance

market-leading position (see Figure 3.10). This prediction held in 2014 when Santander improved the attractiveness of its offer. Lloyds Bank suffered a loss of 103,704 customers in the last quarter of 2013—the largest net loss among the leading banks.

Pharmacy Retailing in Chile

The pharmacy market in Chile is highly concentrated, with three main pharmacy chains dominating the market: (1) Farmacias Cruz Verde with 40 percent share, (2) Farmacias Ahumada with 30 percent share, and (3) Salcobrand with 25 percent share. Together they represent approximately 95 percent of pharmacy sales (compared with about 50 percent of pharmacy sales for the top three U.S. drugstores). As a result, 90 percent of the Chilean population shops in one or more of these pharmacy chains.

In 2008, however, the industry suffered a significant blow when it was accused of collusion to elevate prices of high-demand drugs. As a result, the image for the entire industry transformed from one of healing to one of manipulation. This damaged the brand image of each of the big three pharmacy chains.

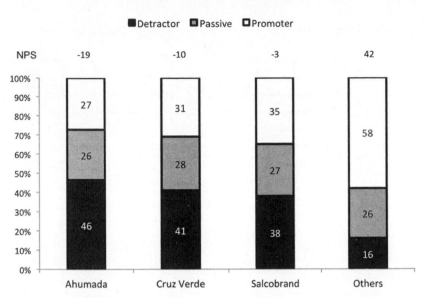

FIGURE 3.11 A Large Percentage of Customers for the Top Three Pharmacies Were Detractors

To understand both the short- and long-term effects of this blow to the industry, we conducted an examination of the market using the Wallet Allocation Rule framework. As a point of comparison, we also measured traditional performance measures to determine their comparative efficacy.

Although penetration of the most powerful firms is extremely high, a market study was still necessary to determine whether customers would penalize the big brands. Conventional research analytics indicated early on that a dire situation was unfolding for the big firms (see Figure 3.11).

Based on NPS levels, the top three firms were headed in the wrong direction. By contrast, small local pharmacies (that comprise only 5 percent of the market) were faring much better based on NPS levels. Given these findings, the big firms were believed to be in real trouble with market share loss on the near horizon.

Nonetheless, despite strong evidence that the scandal did, in fact, cause a significant blow to each firm's image, sales for the big three pharmacies remained very good. To understand why there were no serious consequences (in terms of sales), we used the Wallet Allocation Rule approach to determine what was driving the customers' share of wallet allocations. Comparing the drivers of share of wallet with the drivers of NPS, the differences were striking.

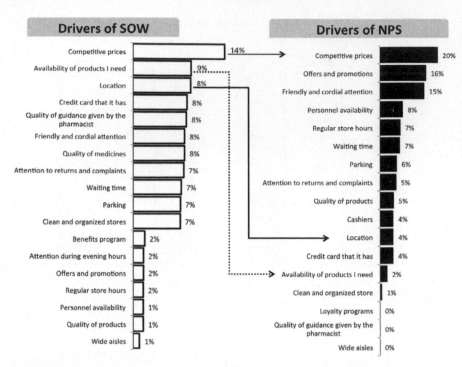

FIGURE 3.12 Drivers of Share of Wallet versus Drivers of Net Promoter Score for Cruz Verde

The top drivers of share of wallet for each of the top three firms were specific to their unique business models. For example, Cruz Verde's share of wallet is driven by three things: competitive prices, stock availability, and store location. Two of the top three drivers of share of wallet using Wallet Allocation Rule, however, are found to have very little effect using a model explaining NPS (see Figure 3.12).

Most of the smaller competitors are out of customers' consideration sets because they cannot meet the store location and stock availability needs offered by Cruz Verde. As a result, the fact that these smaller pharmacies have higher NPS levels is irrelevant. They don't meet the most important criteria driving Cruz Verde's customers' share of spending with pharmacies.

Based on the results of the Wallet Allocation Rule analysis, it is easy to see that the scandal affected the customer satisfaction levels but did so equally across the three biggest competitors. Given this, benchmarking average NPS levels is unlikely to offer useful insight into future share. This occurs in large part because the drivers of NPS do not predict share of wallet. That does not mean that having satisfied customers who are willing to promote the brand is unimportant. However, if the goal is improved customer spending, what matters most are the drivers of share of wallet.

DIY (Do-It-Yourself) Retailing in France

In France, the do-it-yourself (DIY) home improvement market is well established. The market grew 21 percent between 2004 and 2012. Despite the economic crisis that plagued global markets—which led to a flat sector growth rate in 2013—DIY remains the highest expenditure for household equipment, with the average household spending of €800 (approximately $1,000) per year.

These figures attest to the resilience of this sector, largely because 80 percent of the French describe themselves as "committed DIYers" who embrace completing repairs and enhancements to their homes within a controlled budget. The growth of this DIY customer base adds to the already robust core base of construction, carpentry and contract professionals, and handymen in the market.

Specialized retailers began expanding everywhere in France with the emergence of the competitive DIY retail environment in recent years. On average, a French person routinely visits almost three different DIY chains each year. (The equivalent in the United States would be to have eight in 10 adults shopping at three different DIY stores such as Home Depot, Lowe's, and True Value) on a regular basis.

The most-visited French DIY retails are (1) Leroy Merlin, with 37 percent market share; (2) Castorama, with 19 percent market share; (3) Brico Dépôt with 14 percent market share; and (4) Mr. Bricolage, with 12 percent market share. The top four retailers account for 82 percent of the total market, which demonstrates that this is a highly consolidated market.

The high average number of different DIY stores visited by customers, however, clearly shows that they are not held hostage to any particular retailer. Moreover, as each retailer has roughly the same satisfaction score, this is not a meaningful point of differentiation. It should also be noted that the DIY industry does a better job than other retailers in satisfying its customers—overall satisfaction averages in this industry (7.5) exceed the overall retail average (7.1).

When looking at the drivers of satisfaction across these retailers, the story is basically the same for each: Satisfaction is primarily driven by the range of products offered.

Given that each of the major brands is equally satisfying, then this clearly cannot explain the difference in total sales between the brands—certainly not to the level of disparity we see here, where the market share leader, Leroy Merlin, is three times larger than the third largest brand, Brico Dépôt.

When looking at the drivers of share of wallet, however, it becomes clear that each retailer has a distinct aspect of its offer that draws customers (see Figure 3.13).

In the case of Leroy Merlin, a strong reputation for offering good-quality service differentiates it from its competitors, particularly in terms of advice and support; Leroy Merlin is known for DIY trainings, videos, its documentation center, and an open helpline seven days a week. It is important to note, however, that despite its market leadership, Leroy Merlin's own customers are spending money at competitors as well.

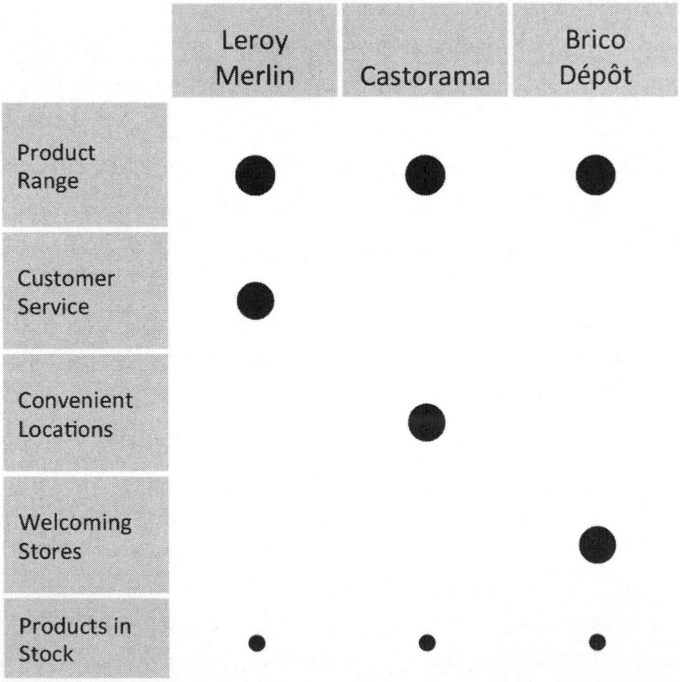

	Leroy Merlin	Castorama	Brico Dépôt
Product Range	●	●	●
Customer Service	●		
Convenient Locations		●	
Welcoming Stores			●
Products in Stock	•	•	•

FIGURE 3.13 Drivers of Share of Wallet for the Top DIY Retailers in France

Castorama is winning business based on the convenience of its locations. In this case, Leroy Merlin is unlikely to compete further with Castorama, because building new infrastructure is difficult, time consuming, and expensive. With improvements to customer service, however, Castorama may become a serious threat to Leroy Merlin.

Brico Dépôt is winning by welcoming customers looking for stores designed for savvy DIYers and professionals. It offers a wide range of products at low prices. This competitive strength, however, is offset by weak product availability and the proximity of its stores. This provides an opportunity for both Leroy Merlin and Castorama to win back more of their customers' spending by incorporating Brico Dépôt's current strengths into their own offerings.

Clearly, the competitive landscape is much more dynamic than is apparent by simply looking at the drivers of satisfaction. An understanding of what drives share of wallet indicates that the French DIY market has the potential for disruption should one of the big three retailers focus on minimizing the reasons customers feel compelled to use a competitor.

Grocery Retailing in Mexico

Mexico's supermarket sector has seen enormous change over the past 10 years. The most notable among these changes is that store formats and layouts have been extensively modified as a trend to big-box stores (e.g., hypermarkets, superstores, etc.) took hold.

These new store formats were significantly larger than those of traditional competitors, whose strategy was based in large part on the convenience of their locations. In response to competition, however, traditional grocery retailers updated their offerings to include both superstores and smaller convenience stores within a few years.

In Mexico, four supermarket chains have large market shares: Walmart is the leader both for its geographical coverage and its market share (47 percent), followed by Soriana (18 percent), Comercial Mexicana (10 percent), and Chedraui (9 percent). In 2013, Walmart showed continued growth through the opening of new stores throughout Mexico and Central America; this was accompanied by the rollout of their e-commerce platform in June 2013. Soriana's image was negatively affected by some political issues 2013, but it has managed to remain financially strong. Meanwhile, Comercial Mexicana experienced a major financial crisis in 2013, making its future uncertain. Finally, Chedraui, which began as a southeast regional player, expanded to have a presence throughout much of the country.

In 2014, we conducted a study among Mexican consumers to understand the competitive landscape of these firms along with general consumer behavior. The findings point to a variety of interesting reasons underlying market differentiation and customers' behaviors beyond just store format.

As predicted by the Wallet Allocation Rule, primary observations regarding the relationship between customer satisfaction and market share show that larger grocery retailers have much lower satisfaction than their smaller competitors. This is because the greater a grocery retailer's market penetration, the more mass market it must become to survive. As a result of its diverse customer base, it provides a less pleasant overall experience, which results in lower satisfaction levels.

In addition, despite higher market shares, customers of these larger players tend to purchase their groceries from multiple retailers. For example, despite significant differences in market shares, both Walmart's and Chedraui's customers allocate nearly identical share of their grocery spending to these brands—36 percent and 37 percent, respectively.

As would be expected, the primary driver of share of wallet for Walmart is price. Walmart, however, is already differentiated well on price. As a result, there is likely little potential in focusing even further on reducing prices.

Instead, Walmart needs to address the reasons that its customers feel the need to use the competition. In Mexico, the drivers of competitors' share differ significantly from their U.S. operations. Walmart in Mexico is losing share of customers' wallets due to a lack of available parking and a lack of product breadth. Although parking may seem to be a minor issue, poor parking is preventing customers from making one-off, small-purchase stops. As a result, these customers go instead to smaller convenience stores. Coupled with Walmart's ability to successfully execute add-on sale items (i.e., customers come in for one thing but end up purchasing additional items), it is clear that the parking problem is resulting in a much larger loss of sales than first meets the eye.

Walmart is also giving up share to its hypermarket competitors because it simply is not offering all of the products its customers want. While matching a hypermarket on its breadth of offerings is likely outside the strategic vision of Walmart, increasing the number of grocery items purchased by its customers most certainly is not. Our findings suggest that Walmart should determine the items its customers are buying elsewhere and identify potential new offerings that it can use to increase the size of its customers' shopping basket.

As this investigation clearly shows, the current traditional drivers of a company's business may not necessarily represent the best opportunities for increased share. For Walmart in Mexico, this means that the best opportunity for improved share of wallet comes from understanding what drives customers to use the competition and using that understanding to minimize competitors' advantages.

Retail Banking in Germany

Retail banking in Germany is a mature business, and almost all of the adult population engages in banking. Germany is home to 2,000 chartered banks, 36,000 bank branches, and about 55,000 ATMs, serving about 66 million adult retail customers. Together, these banks manage €3,090 billion (about $4,230 billion) of deposits. Despite regulation, competition among banks is intense, and managing margins is frequently a challenge.

On top of the existing level of competition, population growth in Germany has leveled off. The need to fight for more market share—without a growing potential customer base for new customers—means growth can be achieved only by stealing away customers from competitors or by garnering a greater share of wallet from existing customers.

There are "three pillars" of German banking: savings banks (*Sparkassen*), cooperative banks (*Volksbanken* and *Raiffeisenbanken*), and private banks. After the 2008 financial crisis, the *Economist* observed, "Two of the pillars—the 423 savings banks and 1,116 cooperative banks—have come through the crisis with barely a scratch so far."[10]

Although the assessment of the *Economist* is correct in terms of the bad loan problems that plagued other financial institutions during the financial crisis, the competitive reality for German savings banks and cooperative banks is not as positive as portrayed.

Savings and cooperative banks combined manage a vast, but declining network of 25,000 branches across the country. It is important to note that for the most part, these institutions are not competing with one another. Most savings and cooperative banks focus on their region; regional savings banks do not compete with other regional savings banks, and cooperative banks typically do not compete with each other across demarcation lines.

Over the past 15 years, direct banks (i.e., Internet banks) have acquired 13 million customers, many of which are still customers of their local savings or cooperative bank. Today, one-third of savings bank customers have a relationship with at least one other bank—for the most part, with a direct bank or with small-footprint consumer finance specialists.

In terms of customer satisfaction, savings and cooperative banks rank at the top among German financial institutions. Nonetheless, despite their higher satisfaction ratings, they are losing pieces of their customers' business to new direct banking competitors.

On the one hand, customers choose savings and cooperative banks in large part because of their convenient branch locations, excellent traditional banking services, and multichannel access to accounts. On the other hand, the drivers of share of wallet for their Internet competitors are top-of-class products and services (for those solutions that they offer) and flawless account management.

Direct banks have recognized that to gain a greater share of customers' wallets, they must work to overcome some of the competitive strengths of savings and cooperative banks. To do this, direct banks expanded their offerings beyond short-tenure high-turnover products (consumer finance, investment accounts, and payments) to include banking products such as primary checking accounts, savings accounts and mortgages, which are the "home turf" of savings and cooperative banks.

Clearly, savings and cooperative banks must work to maintain an advantage in these core banking services. For savings and cooperative banks to gain greater share of wallet with their customers, they must address the reasons their customers are using these direct bank competitors. This means providing state-of-the-art online banking, bill pay, fund transfer, and flawless execution. Of course, this is all easier said than done, even for some of the world's most established financial institutions, because superior delivery means dovetailing services across in-branch and online channels.

The good news for savings and cooperative banks is that there are currently three important market barriers that limit the appeal of direct banks. These result in direct banks receiving relatively low share of wallet levels (around 30 percent), and fewer customers describing it as their "main bank."

First, direct banks do not offer the breadth of services required to be considered an all-in-one institution. This shortcoming prevents between 10 and 15 percent of their customers from doing more business with their direct bank.

Second, approximately 25 percent of customers say that having no branch nearby is a reason to limit bringing in additional business to their direct bank. Of course, as broader acceptance of all-remote banking becomes the norm, this barrier is expected to become less important.

Third, more than 20 percent of direct bank customers hold back portions of their money because there are simply not enough ATMs. Cash is still a critical payment instrument in Germany; even if people don't pull out cash, they want to know they could access it if needed. Here too, however, recent changes may be bringing down this barrier. In cooperation with Visa, the largest direct banks have been offering free cash withdrawal from all Visa-branded ATMs.

The competitive realities of the German banking market highlight the problem of a simple reliance on customer satisfaction. Customers can be very satisfied but still give away pieces of their business to competitors. Addressing this requires an understanding of the drivers of share of wallet for both your firm and the competitors your customers also use.

It also shows that mature markets—such as the German retail banking market—are not immune from shifts in share. Clearly, this market is still evolving. Branch bank groups seek to monetize their huge infrastructure investments, while direct banks seek to overcome barriers by taking novel approaches. Even decades after the emergence of the Internet, it has forced established industries such as the German retail banking sector to continue to innovate in the competition for share of wallet.

Grocery Retailing in Brazil

The grocery retail industry in Brazil is a mixture of large national or international chains that compete with many small, localized chains, as well as one or two outlet shops. Because of their size, the largest supermarkets are able to serve broader customer needs than just grocery shopping. For example, in addition to groceries, larger retailers may also offer services such as pharmacy, tobacco shop, lottery, gasoline, bill-pay stations for utilities, and mobile phone payment.

As a result, large chains such as Extra, Carrefour Hyper, Walmart, and Dia represent formidable challengers to smaller grocery retailers such as Cooperative de Consumo (known as Coop). Coop has 28 stores in 10 cities around São Paulo in Brazil. It has more than 1.5 million "cooperative members" (who receive special discounts and other benefits from being part of a consumer cooperative).

Relative to other, larger grocery retailers, Coop receives high customer satisfaction ratings. The problem, however, is that high satisfaction does not translate into high behavioral loyalty among its customers. Coop's customers overwhelmingly divide their grocery spending among multiple grocery retailers. In fact, 77 percent of Coop's customers use at least one other grocer, and 40 percent shop at two or more competitors. The end result of this divided loyalty is that 45 percent of every Coop customer's spending on groceries goes to a competitor.

An examination of the drivers of Coop's satisfaction revealed that the top four drivers of satisfaction are price, the pharmacy (every Coop store has one), the variety and quality of items, and the membership in the Coop. Of course, price is often one of the most important drivers of satisfaction. Moreover, there is no doubt that if Coop could significantly drop prices, price-sensitive customers would buy more from Coop. As a small cooperative grocery retailer, however, Coop has little room for additional price concessions.

When we use the Wallet Allocation Rule approach to determine precisely why customers feel the need to use competitors (i.e., what drives share of wallet), the most important reason turns out to be the ambience and cleanliness of the stores (specifically the store layout and hygiene). This issue does not even make it into the top six drivers of satisfaction!

Given the results of the Wallet Allocation Rule analysis, it is clear that Coop has real opportunities to win a greater share of its customers' business. But a misguided focus on satisfaction alone would not provide the necessary insight into how to grow share of wallet. Of course, satisfaction is clearly important. For Coop, however, the best opportunity to improve satisfaction—offering even lower prices—is expensive, and it is unclear whether increases in sales with lowered prices will offset the loss of margins. Instead, Coop has an opportunity to improve its customer spending levels by enhancing something completely under its control without having to reduce prices further: how its stores look and feel to customers.

Retail Banking in China

The retail banking market in China is composed of various types of commercial banks, including state-owned banks, joint-equity banks, city banks, rural banks, and foreign banks. The market leadership position of the country's five state-owned banks has come under serious threat from competitors. This is occurring during a period of change in a number of market conditions: interest rate liberalization, a slowdown in national economic growth, a softening of profit margins, and aggressive expansion of service-oriented foreign banks.

In China, it is difficult to discern clearly where customers are depositing their money and why. With such a significant unknown, customer relationship management (CRM) has become increasingly important to banks' competitive strategies aimed at attracting customers' deposits and investments.

The glitch with most CRM approaches, however, is that they fail to focus on the correct key performance indicator (KPI). As a result, it is difficult, if not impossible, to achieve real financial success. By and large, traditional approaches focus on satisfaction and miss the main goal of the entire effort: to reap greater share of wallet.

To gain an understanding of what's driving customers' decisions, we undertook a study of retail banks in China. The major banks investigated included China Merchants Bank (CMB, a joint-equity bank) and five state-owned banks: Bank of Communications (BANKCOMM), Bank of China (BOC), Agricultural Bank of China (ABC), Industrial and Commercial Bank of China (ICBC), and China Construction Bank (CCB).

Using a traditional CRM perspective, ICBC is significantly underperforming relative to its competitors because it has the second-lowest average satisfaction level among the major banking players. In terms of market performance, however, ICBC has the highest share of wallet levels of any of the major banks.

It is clear that satisfaction is a poor predictor of share of wallet in the Chinese retail banking sector. Figure 3.14 clearly shows the weak relationship between satisfaction and share of wallet for the largest banks in China. The correlation is a miniscule 0.052 when looking at all banks

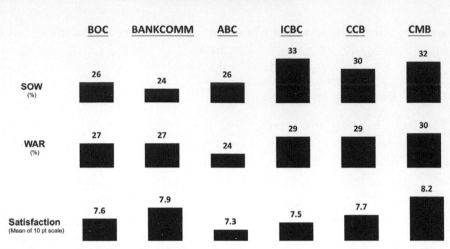

FIGURE 3.14 The Relationship between Satisfaction, the Wallet Allocation Rule, and Share of Wallet for the Largest Banks in China

investigated. In layperson's terms, this means that in excess of 99 percent of the variation in share of wallet is completely unexplained by knowing customer satisfaction levels. By contrast, using the Wallet Allocation Rule results in an extremely strong correlation of 0.924 (the maximum possible is 1.0).

The even more serious issue is that focusing on what drives satisfaction will most likely fail to deliver improved share of wallet. Figure 3.15 shows how the drivers of satisfaction differ significantly from the drivers of share of wallet for banks in China.

Examining the stark difference in results between these approaches reveals how misleading this can be for many banks. BANKCOMM, for example, has three important drivers of share of wallet; two of these drivers in a satisfaction-based approach, however, are the weakest drivers of customer satisfaction (website and convenience across channels). As a result, a satisfaction-based CRM approach would have BANKCOMM focusing on financial advice (a weak share of wallet driver) just as much as customer service (a strong share of wallet driver). This same approach would highlight the website as inconsequential when it is, in fact, the bank's leading driver of share of wallet!

These problems are not isolated to BANKCOMM. The majority of major banks would fail to identify their top three drivers of share of wallet by focusing on satisfaction instead of share. In the case of ABC, on the one hand, its top driver of share of wallet is its sixth-strongest satisfaction

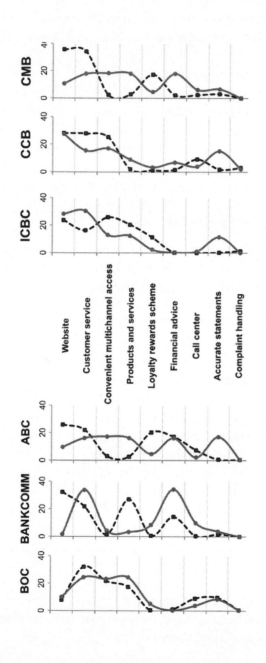

FIGURE 3.15 A Comparison of the Drivers of Satisfaction and the Drivers of Share of Wallet for the Largest Banks in China

driver. On the other hand, its top satisfaction drivers (convenience and range of products and services) are its weakest wallet share drivers. CMB's top share driver is its fifth-strongest satisfaction driver, while one of its strongest satisfaction drivers (financial advice) is among its weakest drivers of share of wallet.

It is obvious that the conventional approach of creating strategy based on absolute customer satisfaction has severe limitations if the ultimate goal is to gain a greater share of customers' banking business. Throughout the China market, the conventional analyses would have wasted time and resources for banks seeking to compete in a market with vast potential and increasing competition. Instead, the Wallet Allocation Rule focuses on what drives customers' share of wallet decisions.

Business Banking in Thailand

Arrow Bank* is a medium-size bank in Thailand with good brand awareness and a long history (established more than 60 years ago). In terms of size, however, it lags significantly behind the top three market leaders. Nonetheless, in addition to individual consumers, Arrow has been able to build a successful business with small and medium enterprises (SMEs) in Thailand. This represents an important customer segment for Arrow, because there are more than 3 million SMEs in Thailand, representing 37 percent of the country's gross domestic product.

Arrow's SME customers are very satisfied with their bank. In fact, the SME unit within Arrow has a world-class NPS of 63 (66 percent of its SME customers are promoters, and only 3 percent are detractors). The top four drivers of Arrow's NPS levels are as follows:

1. Attractive bank fees
2. Offering a variety of SME banking products
3. Easy loan approval process
4. Staff who can answer questions about the bank's products and services

Given these very high scores, it would be easy to conclude that there is little upside potential. After all, 66 percent of customers are classified as loyal using the NPS classification system.

---

*Arrow Bank is a pseudonym. Some details of this case have been disguised to protect client confidentiality without changing the relevant findings.

That conclusion, however, would be far from correct. Arrow has a high percentage of customers who also use competing financial institutions. Worse still, despite high NPS levels, only 38 percent of its SME customers view Arrow as being better than the competition. Twenty percent of SME customers view Arrow as equal to competitors, and the remaining 40 percent see it as worse than the competition.

As a result, Arrow bank captures only 44 percent of its SME customers' share of wallet. Moreover, the average number of banks used by Arrow's SME customers is three.

Arrow Bank's SME customers clearly believe that they need to do business with other financial institutions. Why? An analysis of the Wallet Allocation Rule drivers of share of wallet for SME customers reveals a very different set of drivers:

1. Market coverage/accessibility
2. Overall brand image
3. Branch service quality
4. Easy loan approval process

Given the relatively low share of wallet and high number of competing banks used, there is a great deal of opportunity for Arrow Bank to grow business with its SME customers. However, this will not happen with a simple focus on the drivers of NPS.

The results of the Wallet Allocation Rule analysis revealed that the most important reason that customers do not do more business with Arrow Bank is that it lacks the market coverage of larger institutions. In other words, bigger banks have a bigger footprint (e.g., more branches, bigger ATM networks, etc.), which makes access to banking services much more convenient.

Clearly, Arrow Bank cannot go on a building spree and begin constructing numerous new branches around Thailand if it wants to remain financially strong. Knowing that physical capital is difficult to overcome, however, Arrow Bank should consider adding a few smaller, well-located branches or potentially even microbranches in high-traffic areas. It should also consider ways to use technology to make many of its banking services less location sensitive.

In addition, Arrow needs to actively promote itself as a bank that caters to the needs of small and medium enterprises. Its reputation currently centers on its strength as a consumer bank. Clearly, however, Arrow can provide outstanding service both to individuals and to SMEs.

For Arrow Bank, high NPS scores did not translate into high share of wallet levels, because what makes SME customers happy with Arrow Bank does not at the same time minimize their need to use competing financial institutions. That can be uncovered only by understanding what drives share of wallet.

Retail Banking in South Africa

South Africa enjoys one of the most sophisticated banking industries in the world. Both the retail and corporate services of South African banks compare favorably with the many Western banks, such as Citibank, HSBC, Barclays, ING Bank, Deutsche Bank, ABN Amro, operating in the country.

As with any highly competitive market, however, tough competition has made market saturation a real possibility. The four or five largest banks, as well as a number of new market entrants, have been forced to alter their business models and accept new thinking regarding their services. In particular, banks have been forced to make their services more affordable to attract those without bank accounts (referred to as the "unbanked") given market saturation, which has put downward pressure on margins.

The combination of competitive intensity with a new to banking customer base makes brand positioning critical to success. Moreover, as South African retail banking customers typically use a small number of institutions for their financial needs, it is important that financial institutions have messaging that both stands out and appeals to the majority of consumers.

To address this need, Surety Bank[†] conducted a study of South African banking customers to gain insight in the drivers of their banking attitudes and behaviors. Upon completing the study, however, they were less than thrilled with the findings. The overwhelming number one driver of satisfaction with a financial institution was trust. The rest of the drivers were weak and undifferentiated.

[†] Surety Bank is a pseudonym. Some details of this case have been disguised to protect client confidentiality without changing the relevant findings.

The problem with this finding is that managers at Surety Bank recognized this one simple fact: No one puts their money in a bank that they do not trust. Furthermore, as South Africa is a very sophisticated banking market, virtually all of the major banks in the market meet this standard.

To gain a better understanding of what drives "share of mind," Surety Bank applied the Wallet Allocation Rule to analyze its brand image attributes with the South African banking market in much the same way as it would use the rule to gauge the drivers of share of deposits for its banking customers. On one level, the Wallet Allocation Rule analysis confirmed the initial findings, revealing that the most important factor was still trust. But the second most important driver was simplicity—specifically, that the bank made it simple for customers to use and understand its services. In addition, they wanted a bank that was involved in their communities.

These issues made perfect sense, particularly given the large new to banking segment of the population. More important for Surety Bank executives, it pointed the bank to the key elements of its messaging to prospective customers.

Clearly, Surety Bank has many other opportunities to improve the share of deposits it receives from its customers. Only by first defining a clear and attractive brand positioning, however, would it be given the chance. To grow share of wallet with customers, Surety Bank first had to attract them.

Retail Banking in Turkey

The retail banking sector in Turkey is a changing landscape that faced difficulty during the economic crises of the late 2000s and early 2010s. The dominant institutions in the Turkish banking sector are composed primarily of private and state-owned public banks.

The five largest banks are a mix of both private and public banks: Türkiye Iş Bankasi (Iş Bank), Yapi ve Kredi Bankasi (Yapi Kredi), Garanti Bank, Akbank, and Ziraat Bank. Together, they have combined assets greater than the remainder of the Turkish banking market. As a result, most of the market competition is not between these top five and the remainder of the market. Rather, the toughest competition is between the top five banks as they fight to win share from one another.

In such a competitive environment, managers anywhere in the world would be expected to readily embrace approaches they believe can provide them with a competitive advantage. Turkish banks are no different and have whole-heartedly accepted satisfaction and NPS systems into their marketing and development functions.

Iş Bank (formerly a national bank) is the largest bank in terms of assets in the country. Of the top banks, it has the highest satisfaction ratings, has the highest NPS levels, and is tied for the highest average share of wallet among all its competitors.

At the same time, Garanti Bank—the third-largest bank in terms of assets in the country—is also tied for highest average share of wallet. It, however, has the lowest satisfaction and NPS scores of the top five banks (see Figure 3.16).

As this example clearly demonstrates, high satisfaction and NPS levels are no guarantee of high share of wallet. Of course, this is not to suggest that focusing on creating satisfied customers willing to recommend the brand is unimportant. It most definitely is. But it is not necessarily a good guide for improving share of wallet. In fact, our research finds that not only are the drivers of share of wallet and the drivers of satisfaction different but the drivers of wallet share also differ significantly from bank to bank (see Figure 3.17).

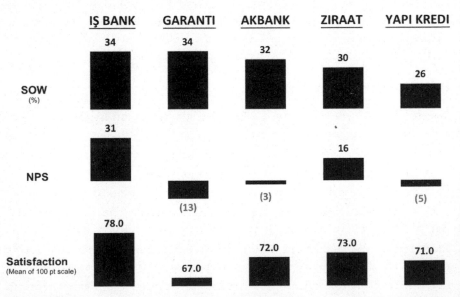

FIGURE 3.16 The Relationship between Satisfaction, Net Promoter Score (NPS), and Share of Wallet for Banks in Turkey

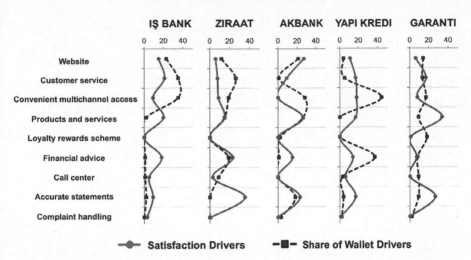

FIGURE 3.17 A Comparison of the Drivers of Satisfaction and the Drivers of Share of Wallet for the Largest Banks in Turkey

The drivers of share of wallet for Iş Bank are focused on multichannel convenience (tied for fifth as a driver of satisfaction), customer service (the top satisfaction driver), and website utility (the fourth-highest satisfaction driver). Equally important for Iş Bank is that efforts to drive satisfaction would be largely split across six drivers, but to drive share the focus would be limited to the three described earlier.

For Garanti Bank, despite having relatively lower satisfaction levels, the bank shares the top spot for highest average share of wallet. This is largely driven by its loyalty reward schemes and the convenience of its locations. Its products, however, are the most powerful drivers of satisfaction.

Ziraat Bank reflects the most dramatic case of satisfaction drivers differing from share of wallet drivers amongst Turkey's largest banks. If Ziraat Bank were to follow a model solely based on driving satisfaction, it would see virtually no financial gain. Ziraat's top driver of satisfaction has a 0 percent impact on driving share of wallet. Similarly, its top driver of wallet share (customer service) would likely have been ignored altogether as it represents the fifth strongest satisfaction driver.

In the case of Akbank, a satisfaction model would have served the bank reasonably well—three of the top four share drivers were also top satisfaction drivers. The top driver of share of wallet (multichannel convenience), however, was last in explaining satisfaction and would have likely been ignored altogether. Similarly, a greater focus would have been placed on financial advice to improve satisfaction despite this attribute having only a 1 percent impact on explaining share of wallet.

Finally, a satisfaction based model for Yapi Kredi would require a focus on four things: customer service, multichannel convenience, products and services, and accurate statements. Only two attributes, however, explain most of customers' share of wallet behavior among Yapi Kredi customers: convenience (a top satisfaction driver) and financial advice (the median satisfaction driver).

In terms of driving share of wallet across the market, the landscape is dotted with many opportunities to grow wallet share that will not be visible in models focusing solely on improved customer satisfaction scores. Convenience is a strong share driver for each of the top five institutions, but it drives satisfaction for only one (Yapi Kredi). Strong website utility is a modest to weak satisfaction driver for each of the top five, but it is a strong wallet share driver for all except Yapi Kredi. Products and services are a universal driver of satisfaction but drive share only for Akbank. Banks that create satisfied customers through things such as financial advice (Ziraat) aren't necessarily the ones benefitting financially from them (Yapi Kredi).

As a result, bank managers in Turkey need to clearly understand what really drives wallet share and what drives only satisfaction. Although both are important, only one drives growth.

Retail Banking in MENA (Middle East and North Africa)

The Gulf Region within Middle East and North Africa (MENA) is widely seen as the region's financial center. It is ranked as one of the wealthiest sectors worldwide. Since 2010, an upswing in the sector has led to increased investments aimed at improving bank offerings, bringing them into closer alignment with those in more developed markets.

This has ultimately resulted in the financial services market becoming one of the most competitive in the entire MENA region. With increased investment comes pressure to succeed in a competitive landscape because capital-liquid investors want to see a return on investment from the managers running the institutions in which they invest.

As managers face increased responsibility, measurement systems have become crucial barometers for performance. Many competitive measurement systems are emblemized by scorecards that contain topline financial information alongside customer metrics such as the NPS.

Over the past half-decade, many scorecard systems in the region have come to rely on NPS systems aimed at enhancing the customer experience.

	Drivers of Share of Wallet (SOW)	Drivers of Net Promoter Score (NPS)
Current Account and Savings Products	42.0%	0.3%
Banking Services through Mobile Application	13.0%	12.0%
Branches	12.0%	18.0%
Fixed Deposits	9.0%	13.5%
Any Type of Credit Cards	9.0%	17.0%
Call Center	8.0%	17.0%
Internet Banking Services	4.0%	15.0%
ATM Services	3.0%	7.2%
Subtotal Products	*60%*	*30.8%*
Subtotal Products	*40%*	*69.2%*

FIGURE 3.18 Drivers of Share of Wallet versus Drivers of NPS

Wanting to examine the attributes critical to driving customer recommendation behavior, bank managers have honed in on eight measures they believe to be important (see Figure 3.18).

Touch points (i.e., interactions between the customer and the bank) are typically determined to be the most important driver of NPS. In fact, it has more than double the impact of bank products and services on NPS. Therefore, if the goal is improved NPS, it is clear where managers must focus their resources and energy.

Bank managers are finding, however, that improved NPS scores are not resulting in the financial returns that they expected. Our research revealed that the focus on touch points is unlikely to result in customers allocating a greater share of their business to banks in MENA. Touch points deliver customer satisfaction, but products deliver share of wallet.

In fact, not only would selecting improvement opportunities based on the drivers of NPS fail to deliver financial results, our research finds that for banks in the Gulf region, there is actually a negative correlation between drivers of recommendation and the drivers of share of wallet.

The overwhelming top driver of share wallet ranks last among elements that drive customers' likelihood to recommend. Therefore, bank managers in the Gulf region who make changes to improve NPS without understanding the competitive landscape may see two unwanted outcomes: (1) failure to grow their customers' share of wallet and (2) having the happiest but least financially rewarding customers the market has to offer.

Conclusion

As these stories from around the world make clear, a misguided pursuit of satisfaction and NPS is unlikely to result in improved financial performance. This should not be taken to mean that satisfaction is not important. To be crystal clear, measuring, modeling, and managing customer satisfaction is more important than ever.

But if the goal is improved share of wallet, then traditional satisfaction and NPS approaches won't cut it. These measures must be put in context of the real-world choices that customers make each and every day. This is best done by applying the Wallet Allocation Rule framework and using it to identify what really drives customers' decisions to allocate more (or less) of their wallets to the brands they use.

4

Customers as Assets

Maybe there is no profit on each individual jar, but we'll make it up in volume.[1]

—Lucille Ball, Emmy- and Golden Globe–award winning comedian, model, and actress

Managers tend to obsess about their satisfaction (or Net Promoter Score [NPS]) levels. One of the first questions managers always ask us is, "What can we do to improve our score?"

Our answer seldom makes them happy. "If all you care about is the score, then cut your prices. Your scores will definitely go up."

In fact, if you simply ask customers what the firm can do to make them happier, you can be certain that lowering price will be the most common answer. Everyone likes a bargain. Bargain prices, however, aren't always good for business.

Although this might sound obvious, it is not often seriously appreciated by managers in their quest to improve satisfaction and NPS levels. Rather, high satisfaction and NPS levels are typically treated as the end goal, with the assumption that good things will happen as a result. And to help make sure that scores go up, employees' bonuses are often tied to achieving them.

Continually devoting resources to improve satisfaction and NPS, however, has a dark side. Research shows that even when these efforts result in improved sales—which is by no means guaranteed—the return on the investment, after accounting for the cost of these efforts, is frequently near zero or even negative.[2] If left unchecked, the consequences can be disastrous.

An unfortunate example of this is HomeBanc Mortgage Corporation. HomeBanc, an Atlanta-based financial institution, began in 1929 originally under the name Home Federal Savings & Loan. For most of its history, it was a small company. By 2005, however, the company had grown to become a 1,200-employee, multistate institution.[3]

HomeBanc's growth was driven by a focus on generating repeat business and referrals. The target market was home buyers because these customers were much more likely to be referred by real estate agents and home builders.[4]

To encourage referrals, HomeBanc focused on improving its NPS. It continuously surveyed its customers and used the data to rank all of its sales teams on a monthly basis.[5] To demonstrate management's commitment to NPS, bonuses and promotions were tied to achieving specific NPS levels.[6]

The result was that HomeBanc had the highest NPS level of any mortgage bank in the United States.[7] HomeBanc's NPS level was remarkably high—in excess of 80 percent. By contrast, the industry average was 3 percent.[8]

The outstanding NPS performance resulted in HomeBanc being prominently featured in the first edition of the book *The Ultimate Question* written by Fred Reichheld, the creator of the NPS. To quote the book, "From the beginning, HomeBanc's secret was to identify the customers most likely to end up in that magic sector [i.e., high-profitability promoters]."[9]

Moreover, "HomeBanc has effectively eliminated bad profits by offering a money-back guarantee."[10] To help make sure that customers never asked for their money back, employees faced stiff penalties if they did. Specifically, if a customer invoked the money-back guarantee, the HomeBanc employee involved in the transaction was typically "counseled" and deemed ineligible for any bonus that year. If it happened more than once, the employee was likely to be fired.[11]

Of course, this gave every incentive for employees to make certain that all went well when they reviewed potential homeowners' loan applications. After all, customers are far more likely to be dissatisfied (and consider it a major incident) if they are denied a loan.[12]

The result was that HomeBanc didn't just eliminate bad profits—it eliminated profits entirely! At the same time that *The Ultimate Question* was hitting bookstores in 2006, HomeBanc was hemorrhaging money. By 2007, HomeBanc had filed for bankruptcy protection and ceased operations shortly thereafter.

For those nostalgic for HomeBanc, however, the name was too good to die. CNBS Financial Group acquired the rights to the name from the defunct Atlanta-based company.[13] Let's hope the future for the new HomeBanc will be different than its predecessor.

The Wallet Allocation Rule Is Not a Panacea

Unfortunately, the HomeBanc story, although tragic, is not unique. In fact, in our first book, *Return on Quality* (with Roland Rust and Anthony Zahorik) published in 1994, we noted several other similar high-profile catastrophes: The Wallace Company, Florida Power & Light, Centennial Medical Center, and IBM.[14] At the time, each of these firms had offered some of the most highly regarded customer service programs in the world. And each met with disastrous consequences.

Fortunately, several of these companies have recovered from their self-inflicted wounds. The Wallace Company—the first small business to win the Malcolm Baldrige National Quality Award—did not.[15] Its market share increased from 10.4 percent to 18 percent. Unfortunately, it was losing $300,000 per month.[16] As a result, it was forced to declare bankruptcy shortly after winning the award and went out of business.[17]

As these business tragedies make clear, managers should never use the pursuit of higher satisfaction or NPS scores to justify making bad business decisions. The same is true for the pursuit of greater share of wallet.

Although the Wallet Allocation Rule makes it possible to strongly link satisfaction (and other commonly used customer loyalty metrics) to share of wallet, greater share of wallet is not a panacea. Managers must make sure that efforts to improve their brand's rank will result in not just greater share of wallet, but also in a positive return on investment.

Where the Money *Really* Comes From

Loyalty consultants typically claim that loyal customers bring in loads of extra money through numerous avenues. The most typically claimed benefits of loyalty are as follows:[18]

1. Lower costs to serve
2. Higher margins (i.e., less price sensitivity)
3. Word of mouth
4. Retention
5. Higher spend (i.e., higher share of wallet)

In fact, based on the charts consultants present of these supposed benefits, you would think that these claimed benefits bring in loads of extra money and that they were all basically equally important.[19] Sadly, that is not the case. In fact, the first two supposed benefits aren't even true.

If managers want to make a positive return on their investments to enhance the customer experience, they first need a clear understanding of where the money really comes from. So let's begin by debunking two of the myths of loyalty: (1) loyal customers cost less to serve, and (2) loyal customers are less price sensitive.

We already debunked these myths in our earlier book, *Loyalty Myths*[20] (with Terry Vavra and Henri Wallard). Unfortunately, like a monster in a horror film, these myths are hard to kill despite evidence conclusively proving them to be false.

Myth: Loyal Customers Cost Less to Serve

The argument that loyal customers cost less to serve is this: "As the company gains experience with its customers, it can serve them more efficiently."[21]

We will be the first to admit that this sounds completely plausible, which is why this myth is so tough to squash. The flaw in this theory is the belief that loyal customers behave the same as their less loyal counterparts do.

The fallacy of that is clear. Real loyalty requires different behaviors. And although there are lots of good customer behaviors for companies associated with loyalty, being easier to serve isn't one of them. Why? Companies may know more about their loyal customers, but loyal customers also know more about the companies. As a result, they may be more demanding of the company through better knowledge of the inner workings of the system. This allows them to seek recourse for what they believe to be inadequate treatment, and they are more likely to receive perks from the relationship, which cost money to administer and fulfill.

Moreover, research conclusively proves this to be the case. Eminent professors Werner Reinartz and V. Kumar conducted in-depth research into several firms to examine the impact of loyalty on the cost to serve customers. Their findings were published in both the *Harvard Business Review* and the *Journal of Marketing*.[22] In no case could they find an example of loyal customers costing less to serve. In fact, when there was a cost difference for a company, the relationship was reversed: Loyal customers cost more to serve.

Myth: Loyal Customers Are Less Price Sensitive

Loyal customers are also widely reported to be less price sensitive—even willing to pay a premium to do business with the company. The argument goes like this: Loyal customers "will often pay a premium to continue to do business with you rather than switch to a competitor with whom they are neither familiar nor comfortable."[23]

That statement is probably true, but it is also totally misleading. The deception is in the qualifier "rather than switch to a competitor with whom they are neither familiar nor comfortable." In other words, "I would be willing to pay more than go someplace I don't know or like."

But is that the real choice customers face? Almost never! Given that multibrand loyalty is the norm in most industries, customers have somewhere else to go. And one of the easiest ways to get them to go there is to charge them a price premium.

The reality is that loyal customers know when prices are good or bad relative to the norm. That's one of the benefits to customers for their loyalty—they know a good deal when they see one. As a result, loyal customers tend to be more price sensitive, not less.

Let's return to the research of professors Reinartz and Kumar. In no case could the professors find an example of loyal customers paying a higher price for the same bundle of goods. If there was a price difference, the relationship was reversed—loyal customers paid less.[24]

Moreover, we've taught our most loyal customers to be price sensitive. As an article in *The Washington Post* notes, "In a subtle shift of marketing tactics, some retailers have stepped up coupon offers directed at their most loyal customers in a bid to attract repeat visits from big spenders.... Eager to wean themselves from discounts for the masses, retailers hope more targeted coupons will limit big bargains to a pool of their best customers."[24]

Word of Mouth

There is no question that positive word of mouth is an important element for a firm's ability to attract new customers. In fact, for many entertainment-related industries (e.g., movies, television shows, nightclubs, etc.), positive customer "buzz" is essential to success.

The Internet and social networks in particular have heightened managers' attention to the potential power of word of mouth. With the help of technology, one person has now the potential to reach hundreds, thousands, and sometimes even millions of people. Moreover, referrals from individual customers tend to have more credibility with prospective customers than company-sponsored advertisements.

As a result, customers' willingness to recommend the brand has become one of the most important metrics that managers use to measure and manage customer loyalty (second only to customer satisfaction).[26] This in large part fueled the adoption of the NPS by many companies. For most businesses, however, the effect of word of mouth on customer acquisition is far less than managers tend to believe.

First, let's begin by examining the relationship between a customer's stated likelihood to recommend a product and the actual adoption of that product by members of his or her social network. Clearly, there is a seductive logic to the idea that customers' willingness to recommend a firm or brand to friends leads to increased sales. We can all think of times that we have tried a new restaurant, seen a new movie, or bought a new product based on the recommendation of friends and family. But does customers' willingness to recommend a firm or brand to friends in their social network really lead to a significant increase in sales? That's precisely the question we wanted to find out for ourselves.

Using data provided by a large U.S. telecommunications provider for 791 customers and their corresponding telephone network (11,552 individuals), we investigated the relationship between customers' willingness to recommend via word of mouth a new product they had purchased and the adoption of that same product by members of their social network.[27] What we found was surprising. A customer's willingness to recommend the product had no significant impact on a potential customer's likelihood to adopt the product.

To see if other factors played a role, we also examined two elements that research has shown influences the role of word of mouth on new product adoption: (1) how recently the product was adopted by the customer (new customers are shown to be more influential) and (2) the strength of the social connection (as measured by communication time). Interestingly, none of these variables demonstrated a statistically significant relationship with adoption of the product when examined individually.

Only by examining the interaction of these variables simultaneously (i.e., recommend intention, recency of adoption, and strength of social connection) was it possible to identify a relationship to product adoption. Specifically, we found that recommend intention predicts new product adoption only when two conditions are met: (1) recommending customers have recently adopted the service themselves (as opposed to being longer-term users of the product), and (2) potential customers are in frequent contact with recommending customers.

Our findings point to the difficulty in translating social networking, recommend intention, and product adoption into a coherent marketing effort. Our results indicate that measuring word of mouth intentions on their own may not be predictive in product adoption by other potential customers. So although knowing your customers' willingness to recommend your brand is important, it is clear that other factors must be taken into consideration and measured when using this particular metric.

Second, let's look at *actual* word of mouth (as opposed to *intention* to recommend) on customer acquisition and profitability. One of the primary drivers of word of mouth is customer satisfaction, with most positive or negative word of mouth occurring at the extremes (either very highly satisfied or dissatisfied).[28] Most of us inherently know this to be true.

What is surprising, however, is that positive word of mouth is three times more common than negative word of mouth.[29] Clearly, negative word of mouth is bad, but it doesn't reflect the majority of customers' discussions about the brands and companies they use.

The question of overriding importance to managers is, "How does this translate into new sales?" Research into word of mouth and customer acquisition finds some unusual things. For one thing, it doesn't have the effect you would expect. For example, given that the success of movies and television shows is in large part based on generating buzz among potential viewers, you would expect word of mouth to be critical to a show's success. Research, however, finds that word of mouth volume doesn't show a consistent relationship to television ratings.[30]

Even more unexpected, research finds that word of mouth activities from loyal customers do not generate additional sales to new customers. Really! So the common argument that increasing customer loyalty results in increased customer acquisition from referrals isn't proving to be true. Instead, research finds that new customers generated by word of mouth come from referrals by nonloyal customers.[31]

If all this leaves you wondering how to make word of mouth pay off, you are not alone. What is clear is that the journey from customer willingness to recommend to gaining new profitable customers is not straightforward. Research by professors Kumar, Petersen, and Leone, reported in the *Harvard Business Review*, sums up the problem this way:[32]

> The number of both companies' customers who said they intended to recommend the firm to other people was high, but the percentage who actually did was far, far lower. While 68% of the financial services firm's customers expressed their intention to refer the company to other people, only 33% followed through. Fully 81% of the telecom's customers thought they'd recommend the company, but merely 30% actually did. What's more, very few of those referrals, in either case, actually generated customers (14% at the financial services firm; 12% at the telecom company). And, of those prospects that did become customers, only 11% of the financial services firm's—and a mere 8% of the telecom company's—became profitable new customers.

This is not to suggest that word of mouth referrals are not valuable. They are! They just aren't nearly as valuable as we've been led to believe.

Customer Retention

For virtually every business, success depends on the repeat business of loyal customers. In fact, it is this recognition that spawned managers' current focus on the customer.

In their seminal *Harvard Business Review* article, "Zero Defections: Quality Comes to Services," consultant Fred Reichheld and esteemed Harvard Business School professor W. Earl Sasser, Jr., triggered a massive shift in companies' strategies by declaring that "reducing defections by 5 percent boosts profits 25 percent to 85 percent."[33] Although these staggering rates of return haven't held up under more rigorous analysis,[34] customer retention is nonetheless one of the most important customer loyalty–related behaviors that drive a company's revenues. In fact, research conducted by professors Gupta, Lehmann, and Stuart finds that a 1 percent improvement in customer retention has a 5 percent impact on a firm's total market value. By contrast, a 1 percent improvement in customer acquisition costs corresponds to a 0.1 percent impact on firm value.[35]

Share of Wallet

As we have argued throughout this book, for most firms, more customers change their spending patterns than do customers who completely defect. Therefore, efforts designed to manage customers' spending patterns with a firm tend to represent far greater opportunities to a firm than simply trying to maximize customer retention rates.

McKinsey & Company argues that focusing on customers' spending patterns to improve customers' share of wallet can have as much as 10 times greater value to a company than efforts to improve retention alone.[36] Our own research similarly supports the far greater impact of share of wallet relative to retention for industries in which customers tend to use multiple brands within the same category.[37]

As this review of the economics of loyalty makes clear, loyal customers bring in greater revenue through three primary means: customer acquisition through word of mouth, improved customer retention rates, and improved share of category spending (i.e., share of wallet). Of these three, share of wallet presents by far the greatest opportunity to grow revenues.

The problem for managers has always been identifying what it takes to grow share of wallet, particularly given that the relationship between share of wallet and metrics such as satisfaction and NPS has been extraordinarily weak. The Wallet Allocation Rule solves this problem. For the first time, managers can easily and accurately determine what it really takes to drive share.

Revenue ≠ Profits

Managers must always remember that increasing revenue is not the same thing as increasing profitability. We forget this at our peril.

The first thing to recognize is that not all—even most—customers are profitable. An examination of customer profitability invariably reveals that although organizations will always have some highly profitable customers, they are also likely to have some highly unprofitable customers. For most firms, the top 20 percent of all customers will generate between 150 percent and 300 percent of total profits. The bottom 20 percent will lose 50 percent to 200 percent of total profits. The middle 60 percent just break even (see Figure 4.1). In other words, 80 percent of a typical firm's customers do not provide an acceptable rate of return.[38]

Most companies treat customer revenue as a good proxy for customer profitability. As a result, they tend to focus their attention on their highest revenue customers. Unfortunately, it turns out that revenue is not a good

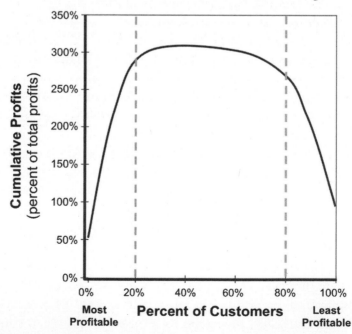

FIGURE 4.1 Typically, the Top 20 Percent of Customers Generate All of a Company's Profits

predictor of profitability. Some of the largest customers also tend to be the most unprofitable. As professors Kaplan and Narayanan of the *Harvard Business School* observe:[39]

> A company cannot lose large amounts of money with small cus-
> tomers. It doesn't do enough business with a small customer
> to incur large (absolute) losses. Only a large customer, work-
> ing in a particularly perverse way can be a large loss customer.
> Large customers tend to be either the most profitable or the least
> profitable in the entire customer base. It's unusual for a large
> customer to be in the middle of the total profitability rankings.

The revenue versus profit issue is particularly problematic for efforts to improve customer satisfaction and NPS. This is because the revenue gained from improvement initiatives frequently does not cover the cost associated with their implementation.[40]

Therefore, managers need to be keenly aware of the warning signs that suggest they are investing money into a black hole. It seems obvious that investments in improving the customer experience need to result in a positive return, but it is easy to get caught up in a *Field of Dreams* men-tality: "If you build it, he will come."[41] Customers may in fact come, but if you are losing money to gain them, it is a Pyrrhic victory.

Short-Term Gain, Long-Term Pain

Some of the most devastating consequences of a blind pursuit of customer satisfaction (and NPS) result from short-termism (i.e., "concentration on short-term projects or objectives for immediate profit at the expense of long-term security").[42] Specifically, managers often focus on achieving near-term goals designed to make customers happier without considering the long-term consequences of their decisions on business performance.

The case of HomeBanc is an excellent example of this problem. The management of the company rightly believed that focusing on better NPS scores would drive greater revenue (in this case, mortgages) to the bank. The problem with this plan is that customer happiness is strongly linked to a positive loan outcome. Unfortunately, not every customer who applies for a loan will have the ability to repay it. When the tough times came (as they always do), those customers who were not properly denied loans became liabilities—so much so that they put the company out of business.

Short-termism runs rampant in companies. In fact, the obsession with near-term profits without an adequate assessment of the long-term risk was one of the primary causes of the financial crisis that resulted in the Great Recession.[43]

Despite the Great Recession, however, the drive to bring in new customers is standard for almost all companies. Moreover, the reality is that the long-term survival of companies is dependent on consistently getting new customers. If left unchecked, however, this obsession with gaining new customers frequently leads to adverse selection (i.e., customers with the highest demand also tend to bring the highest risk to the business). For example, insurers often find that those most in demand for insurance are also at a greater likelihood of experiencing loss. This is why insurance companies are especially fanatical about assessing risk. Unfortunately, most companies do a poor job of assessing long-term risk. In fairness, risks can be notoriously difficult to foresee.

As the Great Recession demonstrates, the societal consequences for large-scale short-termism can be high. Moreover, the negative consequences can be much more than economic losses. A great example of this is the American health care industry.

Patient satisfaction has become an important factor in the financial success of hospitals in the United States. One billion dollars in government payments to hospitals is determined by how patients respond to a 27-question patient satisfaction survey.[44] The logic is simple and intuitive—hospitals should be paid based on performance, and who better to decide than the patients?

In the U.S. government–administered patient satisfaction survey, hospitals are assessed on things such as the following:[45]

- "Area around the room was always quiet at night."
- "Always received help as soon as wanted."
- "Pain was always well controlled."

At first glance, these questions seem perfectly valid. After all, we all want quiet rooms, help as soon as we can get it, and no pain.

Unfortunately, what patients *need* and what they *want* aren't always compatible. In health care, satisfaction and performance is not the same thing. Research shows that patients are much more likely to choose a hospital based on the amenities it offers (e.g., flat-screen televisions, room service, nail salons, etc.) than the quality of care.[46]

The decision about which hospital to use is far from trivial. In fact, it turns out that it is one of the most dangerous decisions we will make in our lives. Research reported in the *Journal of Patient Safety* finds that more than 400,000 Americans die each year from preventable hospital mistakes.[47] This makes hospital error the third leading cause of death in the country![48] Moreover, serious harm to patients from preventable mistakes is 10 to 20 times more likely to occur than death from these mistakes.

For hospitals to be successful, they need patients. The fact that amenities matter more than outcomes has helped fuel a hospital construction boom. Many new hospitals now have rooms and amenities that more closely resemble hotels than the hospitals where our mothers likely gave birth to us.[49]

Of course, the argument could be made that negative outcomes would be reflected in patient satisfaction levels. The truth is that the two actually are related—just in the opposite direction than you would expect.

Research shows that the people who are most satisfied with their doctors are more likely to be hospitalized and accumulate more health care and drug costs.[50] Worse still, they are 26 percent more likely to die than low-satisfaction patients—in other words, for every 100 low-satisfaction patients who die, 126 high-satisfaction patients die.

This isn't because higher satisfaction patients tend to be sicker (at least initially)—in fact, it is the exact opposite. More satisfied patients start out with better average physical and mental health than less satisfied patients. Instead, high satisfaction is actually associated with getting sicker.

Of course, there is a logical reason for this. Focusing on what the patient wants—let's say, minimal pain—may mean that the patient isn't getting what he needs. To quote a recent *New York Times* article on the topic, "Hospitals are not hotels, and although hospital patients may in some ways be informed consumers, they're predominantly sick, needy people, depending on us, the nurses and doctors, to get them through a very tough physical time. They do not come to us for vacation, but because they need the specialized, often painful help that only we can provide."[51]

Of course, doctors and hospitals that get higher satisfaction ratings by giving patients what they want instead of what they need do get a higher share of their patients' health care spending—for as long as their patients are alive. But this situation is clearly not compatible with the Hippocratic Oath.

As these examples of the mortgage and health care industries make clear, it is possible to gain share in the short term by simply ignoring longer-term risks. But bad risks have a way of catching up with you.

Money-Losing Delighters

The most common problem with efforts to improve satisfaction is that the incremental revenue gained is not enough to offset the costs of these initiatives. Often this occurs because price drives satisfaction for a large segment of customers in most industries.

Satisfaction and price are almost always inversely related. As a result, lowering price tends to be one of the easiest ways to improve satisfaction levels (see Figure 4.2).

Unfortunately, the potential to drop prices for most firms is limited. As a result, price-driven satisfaction is typically a difficult strategy to

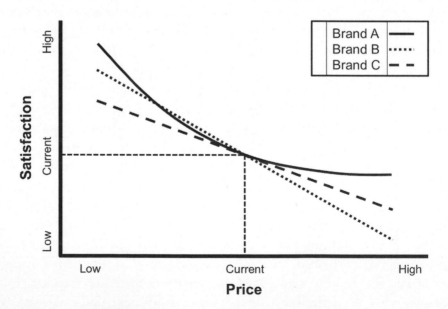

FIGURE 4.2 The Relationship between Price and Satisfaction

maintain. Even small errors can result in huge losses as customers rush to buy below cost.

Many retailers learned this the hard way when working with Groupon. In effect, retailers were promised that deep discounts marketed to consumers through Groupon would drive sales and pay for themselves through cross-sales at the time of purchase and repeat purchases based on satisfaction with the experience.

Without question, Groupon promotions tend to drive sales volume. But as we report in our Harvard Business School case (with Harvard professors Sunil Gupta and Ray Weaver), the happier the experience made customers, the worse the outcome for the retailer.[52] In fact, four of the top six performing offers in terms of satisfaction turn out to be money losers for the merchant, and these are the only offers that consistently lose money for merchants (see Figure 4.3). Because of the high customer satisfaction associated with these offers, however, they generate a huge demand. These four categories account for 50 percent of total Groupon volume!

These findings point to an important truth about the relationship between customer satisfaction and customer profitability. Although satisfaction and profitability are not mutually exclusive, they don't have to be aligned either. Managers typically have many competing alternatives

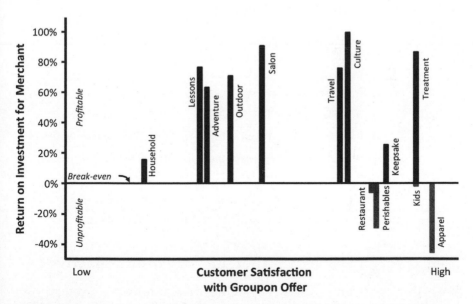

FIGURE 4.3 Customer Satisfaction versus Return on Investment for Various Groupon Offers

for improving satisfaction. Not all of them will be profitable. Furthermore, not all customers can be profitably satisfied. Some are not willing to pay the necessary price for the level of service offered. Other customers demand a level of service that more than offsets any revenue they provide.

The bottom line is that there is no substitute for understanding the profit impact of your efforts to boost customer satisfaction. Armed with this information, managers can make the right—but sometimes difficult—decisions for their businesses.

Aligning Satisfaction, Share of Wallet, Revenue, and Profit

Short-termism and money-losing delighters have the potential to derail any positive impact resulting from strategies designed to improve the customer experience. Fortunately, they don't have to. Following is a three-step process that managers can follow to ensure that efforts to improve the customer experience result in a positive financial return.

Step 1: Use the Wallet Allocation Rule to Link Satisfaction and Share of Wallet

With the Wallet Allocation Rule, step 1 is easy. To link satisfaction (or NPS) to share of wallet simply do the following:

- Survey customers and establish the brands (or stores or firms) that customers use in the category.
- Obtain satisfaction ratings for each brand the customer uses.
- Convert each customer's satisfaction ratings for the brands he or she uses into ranks.
- Use the Wallet Allocation Rule to transform these ranks into estimates of each customer's share of category spending.

Step 2: Align Share of Wallet and Revenue Objectives

Improving the share of category spending that customers allocate to your brand is the primary goal, but share of wallet must always be considered in tandem with the total revenue that customers spend in the category.

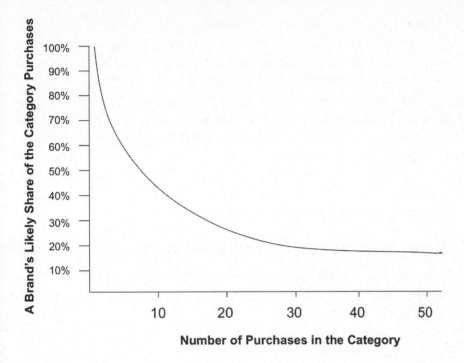

FIGURE 4.4 Share of Wallet Tends to Decline as More Purchases Are Made

Clearly, customers who buy only once in a category give 100 percent of their wallet share to a single brand.

The reality is that customers who spend more in the category are much more likely to divide their spending among multiple brands (see Figure 4.4).[53] The goal, of course, is not to get customers to spend less in the category to raise share of wallet. The goal is to get customers to allocate more of their purchases in the category with your brand.

Therefore, we need to understand share of wallet in the context of the revenue it represents. Not every customer is capable of being a high-revenue, high-share of wallet customer, nor does every customer want to be one. Some customers make purchases in the category so infrequently that unless these customers represent a significant portion of the customer base, servicing and marketing to such customers yields too little in return.

Therefore, at a minimum, we need to segment customers by the volume of business they conduct in the category. Because low-spending customers tend to be much less involved in the category, their needs tend to be very different from high-spenders.

Furthermore, high-revenue customers are almost always in the minority in terms of number of total customers. Strategies that neglect customer differentiation will inevitably tilt the scale toward break-even and unprofitable customers because they represent the majority.

High-category spending, high-share customers represent a company's core customers. The goal must be to create more of them. The only customer group with the necessary resources to move into this group is the high-category spending, low-share customers. The key to making this happen is to have a clear understanding of precisely why these customers choose to use competitors. Improvement efforts must then minimize customers' perceived needs to use the competition.

Step 3: Align Revenue and Profit Objectives

Understanding the relationship between share of wallet and revenue is not enough. As noted earlier, there are lots of ways to grow share while still losing money.

The seemingly logical answer to solve this problem is to ignore revenue and focus exclusively on return on investment (ROI). That, however, is typically not the best solution for a business either. Maximizing ROI often comes from defining the customer pool too narrowly to gain significant market share growth.

Instead the goal should be to maximize the return on each high-potential customer.[54] This shifts the focus from maximizing ROI to maximizing profits. Without overcomplicating this, the key is to determine what is required to address the overriding reasons your customers use competitors and the cost of doing so. These costs are then weighed against the expected financial return.

Conclusion

The Wallet Allocation Rule measures what has generally been considered immeasurable: the impact of improving satisfaction on customers' share of spending and firm revenue. Yet although this linkage to revenue is critical, it isn't sufficient.

Managers must never lose sight of the fact that the end goal is profits, not just revenues. Using the Wallet Allocation Rule to identify opportunities to grow revenues does not justify making bad management decisions.

Improvement efforts must always be treated as investments—their benefits must outweigh their costs. And the reality is that many potential opportunities to improve share of wallet and revenues will never pay off.

It's the manager's job to assess risks and evaluate costs. HomeBanc, the Wallace Company, and a host of other broke but beloved companies[55] serve as a warning for all managers who forget this simple truth.

Growth is easy for firms willing to give their products away—for as long as they remain in business! But to quote Peter Drucker, "It is the first duty of a business to survive."[56]

New Metrics That Matter for Growth

In God we trust, all others bring data.[1]
— *W. Edwards Deming, American engineer, statistician, author,
and esteemed quality consultant*

An astonishing 50 percent of the 3,000 medical treatments that have been studied around the world in controlled, randomized trials are of unknown effectiveness—in other words, we have absolutely no idea how well they work, or if they work at all![2] Worse still, this doesn't mean that the other 50 percent actually work. A study by *Clinical Evidence*, a project of the *British Medical Journal*, finds that only one-third of treatments are likely to be beneficial: Specifically, 11 percent have been shown to be beneficial, and 23 percent are likely to be beneficial. Of the remainder, 7 percent have trade-offs between harms and benefits, 6 percent are unlikely to be beneficial, and 3 percent are likely to be ineffective or even harmful.[3]

These numbers are shockingly bad. How is it possible that an industry filled with highly educated individuals and whose success can be objectively observed in the health of its customers (i.e., patients) would rely on so many unproven treatments? The reality is that ideology and tradition get in the way of medical evidence all the time.[4] In fact, research indicates that an abysmal 15 percent of doctors' decisions are based on factual evidence.[5] To quote Dr. David Newman, director of clinical research at Mt. Sinai School of Medicine:[6]

> Treatment based on ideology is alluring. Surgeries to repair the knee should work. A syrup to reduce cough should help. Calming the straining heart should save lives. But the uncomfortable truth is that many expensive, invasive interventions are of little or no benefit and cause potentially uncomfortable, costly, and dangerous side effects and complications. The critical question that looms for health care reform is whether patients, doctors and experts are prepared to set aside ideology in the face of data. Can we abide by the evidence when it tells us that antibiotics don't clear ear infections or help strep throats? Can we stop asking for, and writing, these prescriptions? Can we stop performing, and asking for, knee and back surgeries? Can we handle what the evidence reveals? Are we ready for the truth?

Because we will all need medical care at some point in our lives, we sincerely hope that the answer to these questions is yes.

Glass Houses and Stones

The current state of management practice is hardly immune to the same issues that plague medicine. In fact, in their seminal *Harvard Business Review* article on the need for "Evidence-Based Management," Stanford University professors Jeffrey Pfeffer and Robert Sutton—while acknowledging the major problems in medicine—argue:[7]

> Managers are actually much more ignorant than doctors about which prescriptions are reliable—and they're less eager to find out. If doctors practiced medicine like many companies practice management, there would be more unnecessarily sick or dead patients and many more doctors in jail or suffering other penalties for malpractice.

Although it is easy to presume some level of incompetence or outright dishonesty, the reasons for the lack of evidence-based management have more to do with being human than anything else. Most of our mistaken beliefs happen because we want to believe in them. And the reasons we want to believe are numerous:

- Personal experience is believed to trump research-based evidence.
- We prefer compelling stories to hard data.
- The truth is often complicated, whereas the myth is typically simple.
- We ignore evidence that contradicts our beliefs, so we only see what we expect to see.
- We like to deliver good news.
- We like to receive good news—and so do our bosses!

Pfeffer and Sutton point to one additional problem, however, that is not a function of being human. There are people—typically with something to sell—who are actually trying to mislead you:

A big part of the problem is consultants, who are always rewarded for getting work, only sometimes rewarded for doing good work, and hardly ever rewarded for evaluating whether they have actually improved things.... If you think our charge is too harsh, ask the people at your favorite consulting firm what evidence they have that their advice or techniques actually work—and pay attention to the evidence they offer.[8]

Their evidence is almost always anecdotal, praising the supposed success stories of their advice or techniques at other companies. The problem, to quote IMD Business School professor Phil Rosenzweig, is that "a good anecdote can be found to support just about anything. If we want to [actually] show that [something] has a major impact on business performance, we have to gather data across companies and look for patterns."[9]

Even when there is some allusion to supporting research, managers can be virtually certain that it has not been vetted in a high-quality, peer-reviewed scientific journal. Adding to the problem, most managers do not know the difference between a management magazine article and a peer-reviewed scientific paper. A simple rule of thumb is that if the article is easy to read, nontechnical, and doesn't have lots of underlying academic theory in the write-up, it is probably not a peer-reviewed scientific journal regardless of how prestigious the university name on the cover.[10]

Of course, this adds to the problem. The fact that scientific papers are often boring and contain lots of Greek mathematical notation further limits managers' interest in them. As a result, the simple and wrong explanation (or as we like to say, "simply wrong" explanation) often wins over the more complex truth. Although managers can blame scientific researchers for writing obscure, difficult-to-read research for the lack of application of these ideas in business, the sad reality is that academic researchers must publish this type of research and writing to advance in their careers. As a result, managers are often forced to wade through some pretty boring papers to uncover important, vetted new ideas to help them grow their businesses.

Nonetheless, managers can and should insist that when consultants present them with a reported "breakthrough" idea, they also prove that these ideas have been scientifically vetted. Anyone can write a "white paper" that far too often passes for proof in companies. The peer review process provides a much higher standard for a reason—it helps weed out bad ideas. And as we have shown, many of the ideas related to customer management and how it links to business outcomes have proved to be very bad indeed.

Must-Have Marketing Metrics

The Wallet Allocation Rule makes it possible for managers to easily link customer satisfaction to share of wallet. But because the rule is based on a company's relative rank, not its absolute satisfaction levels, firms need to add to their Key Performance Indicators (KPIs). The three metrics that every firm using the Wallet Allocation Rule should follow are as follows:

1. Percent first choice
2. Average number of brands used
3. Share of wallet

Percent First Choice

Given that using the Wallet Allocation Rule focuses on rank as opposed to the absolute satisfaction (or Net Promoter Score) level, it is important to monitor performance in a way that corresponds to this new perspective. Managers must do so in a way that is simple enough for their employees to grasp and at the same time reflective of how customers allocate spending with their brand.

A brand's average rank is not easy for either senior managers or frontline employees to interpret, nor is it easy to rally the organization around. This is because we think of ranks as whole numbers—such as first place, second place, third place, and so on. A firm's average rank, however, is almost never a whole number. As a result, it is hard for managers and frontline employees to internalize.

An easy way to get around this problem is to track the percentage of customers who give your brand their highest satisfaction rating among all brands that they use. In other words, is your brand really a customer's first choice, or do customers view your brand as being the same or worse than competitors? Looking at the percentage of customers who rate a brand better than all other competitors correlates strongly with share of wallet (see Figure 5.1). Although the first choice percentage is not quite as

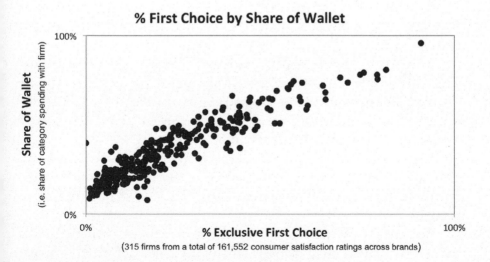

FIGURE 5.1 First Choice Tracks with Share of Wallet

strongly correlated to share of wallet as the complete Wallet Allocation Rule calculation, it provides an easy-to-understand and easy-to-use metric that keeps the focus on where the brand ranks relative to competition.

Average Number of Brands Used

The Wallet Allocation Rule also makes clear that the number of brands used in the category by a customer has a strong impact on share of wallet. As a result, managers need to understand how and where customers allocate their category spending.

Customers have logical reasons for using every brand that they do. Therefore these multibrand users must have certain needs that they perceive are better fulfilled by competing brands. Tracking the number of brands that customers use keeps the focus on reducing customers' perceived needs to use competing brands with the ultimate goal of eliminating competitors from customers' usage sets entirely.

Share of Wallet

Gaining a higher share of customers' category spending is a common goal for managers. But most managers have no idea about the size of the share of wallet customers allocate to their brands and that of their competitors.

To be fair, the data aren't readily available in most industries. After all, companies typically don't share their customers' buying behaviors with their competitors.

Even when share of wallet data is available, it is almost never customer identifiable. This makes it virtually impossible to connect share of wallet information with your brand's customer database. As a result, managers have been hamstrung when developing programs designed to improve their share of customer spending.

Fortunately, it is possible to collect share of wallet information via consumer surveys. Moreover, academic researchers have developed robust systems for aligning and validating survey-based and observed share measures.[11]

Because the Wallet Allocation Rule is all about growing share of wallet, it is important that managers monitor the share of wallet that customers allocate to their brands. It is also important to know the share of wallet that your brand's customers allocate to competitors (which can be easily determined using the Wallet Allocation Rule).

A	Total revenue my customers give to my brand			$	6,000	
B	Average share of wallet my customers give to my brand				÷ 25%	
A/B	Total revenue my customers give to all brands in category			$	24,000	

		Competitors			
		Brand A	Brand B	Brand C	My Brand
C	Average share of wallet my customers give to competitors	10%	20%	45%	25%
D	Total revenue my customers give to all brands in category	x 24,000	x 24,000	x 24,000	x 24,000
C x D	Average spending my customers give to competitors	$ 2,400	$ 4,800	$ 10,800	$ 6,000

FIGURE 5.2 Determining How Much of Your Customers' Money Goes to Competitors

Because share of wallet is a metric that can be translated directly into dollars, it is imperative to understand precisely how much of your customers' money is going into your competitors' cash registers. To do this, managers need to simply do the following (see Figure 5.2):

1. Divide the total sales revenue that your customers give to your brand by the average share of wallet that your customers give to your brand. This will give you the total dollars your customers spend in the category across all brands (yours and competitors).

2. Multiply your customers' total category spending by the average share of wallet your customers give to each of the brands that they use. This will give you the total dollars your customers spend with each competing brand.

With this information, managers get a real understanding of where their customers' money is going. More important, they can discover where significant opportunities exist to take back share from competitors.

Customer Satisfaction

Although absolute customer satisfaction levels do not link to share of wallet, satisfaction itself is not unimportant. Clearly no firm lasts for long without satisfied customers.

Instead, the Wallet Allocation Rule shows that customers' satisfaction levels matter most when put in a competitive context. In the case of the Wallet Allocation Rule, it is relative "ranked" satisfaction that matters.

Satisfaction information in conjunction with other metrics can provide important strategic insight. Two of the most important metrics are

(1) satisfaction's relationship to market share and (2) satisfaction's relationship to being customers' first choice (i.e., their preferred brand).

Working with Harvard Business School professor Sunil Gupta, we developed several strategy matrices that quickly provide managers with insight into the nature of competition in their markets.[12] Next we discuss how this information can be used to guide a company's customer-related strategies.

Satisfaction and Market Share

Used together, satisfaction and market share information provides managers with important insight into the nature of their brand and the markets in which they compete. Remember, the relationship between customer satisfaction and market share is negative in many industry categories. Without a good understanding of the nature of the relationship in your industry, and of where your firm stands vis-à-vis competitors, it is very difficult to effectively manage the customer experience in the pursuit of market share.

The place to begin is with an analysis of your customers' levels of satisfaction with your firm and with your competitors' customer satisfaction levels with these competing firms, as well as your and your competitors' market shares (see Figure 5.3). If one or more firms have high market share and low customer satisfaction, the industry most likely demonstrates a negative relationship between customer satisfaction and market share.

Firms with high share and low satisfaction combinations are what we refer to as mass market brands. These firms have a wide range of customers

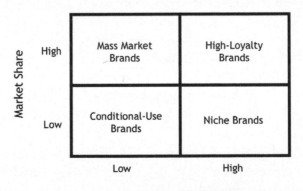

FIGURE 5.3 Customer Satisfaction versus Market Share

with a diverse set of needs that can be met in large part by the firm. But it's impossible for these brands to precisely meet the needs of all or even most customers. As a result, some core benefit, such as price, convenience, or product assortment, needs to be sufficiently strong for customers to believe sacrificing other desired benefits to be worth the exchange. In many categories, this strategy has proved very successful, which is why many mass market brands represent some of the most well-known brand names: McDonald's, Walmart, and Microsoft Windows.

Because mass market brands focus on the general needs of a wide audience, they typically find themselves competing with smaller, more focused competitors that better target the needs of specific segments of customers. These niche brand competitors must have higher satisfaction levels to survive. Yet because these firms target a smaller segment of customers, their market share is relatively low. For example, niche brand fast-food burger restaurants such as Five Guys Burgers and Fries have higher satisfaction levels than any of the big three burger chains (i.e., McDonald's, Burger King, and Wendy's) because of their almost exclusive focus on burgers and fries. Clearly this strategy has proved highly successful for Five Guys, but its limited menu also makes it virtually impossible for the chain to achieve market share leadership.

In some categories, there are brands that exhibit both high customer satisfaction and high market share, which we refer to as high-loyalty brands. For example, Google has consistently received higher customer satisfaction ratings than its competitors in Internet search while capturing almost two-thirds of U.S. search activity. High-loyalty brands, however, are similar to mass market brands in that they face competition from niche brands.

How are these brands able to avoid the relatively poor customer satisfaction score that mass market brands typically receive? It is interesting to note that high-loyalty brands often are found in the technology sector, a dynamic market. Competitive intensity combined with rapidly changing and improving product offerings means that these markets are in constant flux. As a result, customers have not habituated to the products offered. But this is a double-edged sword. Because the markets are in a high state of flux, winners can quickly lose ground—as companies such as BlackBerry have discovered.

Some brands, despite relatively low satisfaction and low market share levels, compete successfully. These conditional-use brands, as we refer to them, succeed either because they uniquely offer items needed to complete the consumer's shopping basket in the category or because some market barrier makes using a preferred brand difficult. For example, many retailers and restaurants compete largely through the convenience of their locations relative to competition.

Given that each quadrant of the satisfaction and market share matrix represents a viable business strategy, simply comparing average satisfaction levels across brands in a category offers little real insight. In particular, if larger share brands are likely to have lower satisfaction than smaller brands, how exactly are managers to compare their performance vis-à-vis competition? In our own experience, managers of some the world's largest brands often benchmark their performance against the highest satisfaction brands in the category despite the fact that their share is often significantly smaller. Moreover, senior executives tend to view these levels as attainable targets for their own firms just because a competitor achieved them.

Consultants often go even farther down this path. It is virtually impossible for managers to go through their employment histories without hearing a management guru expound on how their brands should be more like great—but niche—brands such as Harley Davidson, Disney, Cirque du Soleil, and so on. The underlying argument is that customer expectations are not only set by direct competitors' performance but also established by all firms with which customers conduct business. Although there may be a grain of truth to this argument, most of the time it is not managerially relevant. Whereas learning from the experiences of other firms is beneficial, setting target satisfaction levels based on the performance of niche players is not only unrealistic it's a bad business decision.

So how should a 40 percent market share *Brand A* compare itself to a 10 percent market share *Brand B* in terms of satisfaction? A simple rule of thumb is to compare satisfaction levels of customers that correspond to equivalent market shares for both. In the case of this example, *Brand A* would take its top customers, which constitute 25 percent of its revenue (if it had only those customers it would have 10 percent market share), and compare their satisfaction level with that of *Brand B* (see Figure 5.4). If they are comparable, then *Brand A* is fine. If, however, it is significantly lower, then *Brand A* managers need to assess the risk of losing these customers to competitors and work to mitigate that risk.

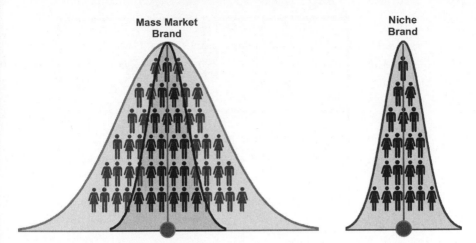

FIGURE 5.4 Comparing Mass Market and Niche Brands
A simple rule of thumb is to compare satisfaction levels of customers that correspond to equivalent market shares for both brands.

Satisfaction and First Choice

The overriding reason for managements' focus on customer satisfaction is because they believe it is a source of competitive advantage. At some level, managers expect high satisfaction levels to cause customers to prefer a brand to competitive alternatives.

Clearly, there is some truth to this. As with all management truisms, however, the devil is in the details. It is quite possible in many categories for a brand to have high satisfaction or Net Promoter Score levels and yet not be a customers' undisputed first choice. In other cases, a brand can be a customer's exclusive first choice but have relatively low satisfaction levels. This presents managers with a real problem—what is a good score?

Part of the problem is a general misunderstanding of how satisfaction (and Net Promoter Score) link to customers' buying behaviors. The absolute scores themselves are almost meaningless. What matters is whether or not the customer rating is higher for your brand than for competing brands. The lion's share of a customer's wallet goes to his first-choice brand. Therefore, it is vital to understand how a brand's satisfaction level translates into a position as the customer's first choice.

By analyzing your customers' levels of satisfaction and their corresponding first-choice selection, you can place each of them into one of

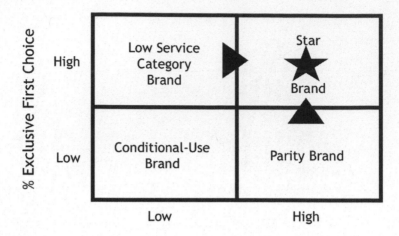

Customer Satisfaction

FIGURE 5.5 Customer Satisfaction versus First Choice

four categories, as shown in the matrix "Satisfaction and First Choice" (see Figure 5.5).

If your customers both are highly satisfied and prefer your brand to all others, you are the star brand in the category. Here the strategy is simple—continue to delight these customers.

At the opposite end of the spectrum are brands that are low in satisfaction and in first-choice preference. This environment gives rise to the conditional-use brands we discussed earlier. The strategy for these brands is to maintain unique items that would be difficult or unprofitable for competitors to incorporate into their offering or to find ways to erect market barriers that make access to a preferred brand difficult.

For those customers whose satisfaction is high but first choice is low, high satisfaction levels are masking customers' real perceptions of the brand. Managers typically tout the fact that customers are highly satisfied, but the reality is that the brand is one of several that the customer uses and views as being basically equivalent, which is why we refer to these brands as parity brands. Although being at parity may sound like no big deal, there are no multiple gold medal winners in business. Rather, you evenly divide your customers' share of spending with your strongest competitors. The strategy for these brands must be differentiation from core competitors—in other words, you must give customers a reason to believe your brand is uniquely better than competitors.

There are also brands that despite low satisfaction still represent customers' first choice. These low service category brands compete successfully either because the category has few competitors or because these brands compete largely on price leadership. These brands can succeed provided sufficient entry barriers for competitors exist or significant price leadership can be maintained. This, however, is an inherently difficult position to maintain. In an era of open access to information, wide access to markets, and easy price comparisons, cost leadership strategies often come at the expense of acceptable financial returns. As a result, competitive markets tend to pressure firms to raise their satisfaction levels to remain customers' first-choice brand.

Key Drivers and Market Barriers

With the Wallet Allocation Rule, managers can easily make the critical link between customer satisfaction and share of wallet. Specifically, relative ranked satisfaction strongly links to share of category spending using the Wallet Allocation Rule.

Of course, the ability to connect rank with share of wallet does not immediately translate into a clear-cut strategy to improve rank and, by extension, wallet share. This requires an understanding of the key drivers of rank as well as the structural barriers in a market that make it difficult for customers to purchase their preferred brand. Next we discuss these two critical issues in making the Wallet Allocation Rule work for your firm.

Key Drivers[13]

When it comes to using the Wallet Allocation rule, the most important question that managers want answered is "Where should I focus my efforts?" Because managers have many potential improvement opportunities, they need to be able to prioritize them based on their potential financial return.

Managers have traditionally relied on key driver analysis to guide them about the most important issues affecting customer satisfaction (or Net Promoter Score). Traditional driver analyses examine the relationship between customers' satisfaction with specific attributes of the service experience and their overall satisfaction levels.

Traditional driver analyses, however, will not work with the Wallet Allocation Rule. With the Wallet Allocation Rule, satisfaction is not measured in a vacuum. What's important here is the rank of a brand's satisfaction level compared with that of its competitors. Specifically, overall satisfaction ratings for all brands that a customer uses are required in order to establish the proper context.

As a result, to understand the drivers of rank, the attributes of the service experience must be determined in relation to the competition. This represents a major departure from traditional driver approaches.

The most comprehensive approach to achieve this is to ask all respondents to rate all brands used on all attributes, then convert the attribute ratings into ranks just as we do with overall satisfaction. Unfortunately, asking a full battery of questions for every brand a customer uses is at times impractical.

When that is the case, managers can still place attributes in a relative framework by presenting customers with a checklist of options rather than having them rate each attribute (see Figure 5.6). This involves using a grid with one column for each brand that a customer uses and one row for each driver attribute. The objective is to have respondents select the brand(s) that perform best on that attribute.

Although this approach cannot provide a set of ranks on the driver attributes that can be run against the overall rank, it is consistent with the philosophy of striving to be number one. Remember, the greatest share of wallet is allocated to the brand that occupies the number one space.

Distinguishing between the drivers of satisfaction and the drivers of rank would be unnecessary if both sets of drivers pointed to the same

	BRANDS USED				
	Brand 1	Brand 2	Brand 3	Another Brand	None
Process Attribute 1	☐	☐	☐	☐	☐
Process Attribute 2	☐	☐	☐	☐	☐
Process Attribute 3	☐	☐	☐	☐	☐
Process Attribute 4	☐	☐	☐	☐	☐
Etc...	☐	☐	☐	☐	☐

FIGURE 5.6 "Share of Best" Grid
Thinking of the brand(s) you currently use, which would you associate with being best in each of the following areas? (Check all that apply.)

opportunities for improvement. That, however, is most definitely not the case. An analysis by Alex Buoye, a coauthor of this book, clearly demonstrates the stark difference between these two types of drivers.[14]

A simple regression analysis revealed that the top driver of satisfaction with grocery retailers was product range (followed closely by customer service). Of course, this makes total sense. Carrying the products your customers want is the raison d'étre for any retailer, especially one dealing in regularly purchased staples, like groceries. If you were to ask a customer why she shops at a particular store, it would not be surprising to hear her say that the store simply has the products she wants. In addition, providing friendly customer service is almost always a good way to boost satisfaction scores; good customer service produces positive sentiment. But if you really think about it, are product range and customer service the main reasons someone decides to shop at a particular grocery store?

By contrast, you probably would be surprised if a customer told you the best thing about the store was its location. The research uncovered that the most important driver of share, however, was in fact the perceived convenience of the location (see Figure 5.7). When comparing stores where one shops, better location doesn't do much to differentiate the satisfied from the dissatisfied customers. In fact, it was dead last among the list of

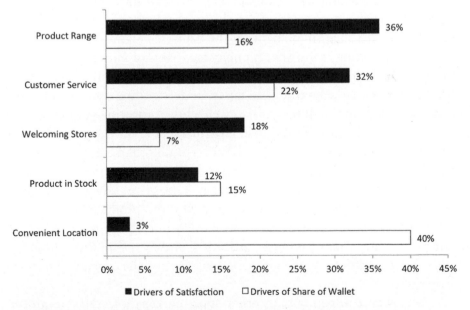

FIGURE 5.7 Drivers of Satisfaction versus Drivers of Share of Wallet

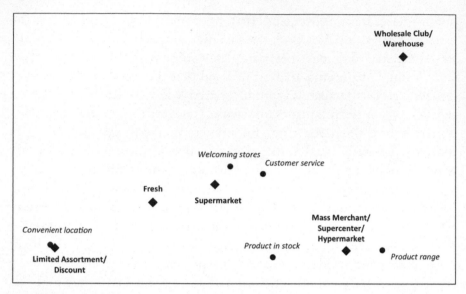

FIGURE 5.8 Perceptual Map of the Drivers of Share of Wallet for Different Grocery Retailers

drivers of satisfaction that were examined! But it makes a huge difference in determining how much one shops there.

A separate analysis grouping retailers into categories based on dominant store formats (supermarket, "fresh," mass merchant, warehouse, limited assortment) sheds more light on the issue (see Figure 5.8).

When looking at the brands one uses, drivers of satisfaction actually form the basis for competitive positioning. It isn't simply about being "better" at one particular thing but rather understanding how to maximize your advantage on the things you do well while mitigating your competitors' relative strengths. Traditional supermarkets (e.g., Kroger, Safeway) and fresh markets (e.g., Whole Foods) are typically characterized by better customer service and more welcoming stores, whereas limited assortment stores (e.g., Aldi) generally have location (and price) advantages. Mass merchants/supercenters (e.g., Walmart) win on product range—not necessarily in terms of groceries specifically, but across multiple retail categories, capturing customers' grocery spending *while* they shop for other goods without groceries necessarily being the reason *why* they shop there.

So, when competing with other supermarkets, a traditional grocer may be able to win back some of its customers' spending by focusing on the things that they both do well. But when competing with a mass merchant, the key driver to be addressed may be quite different. Understanding the key drivers of share requires knowing who your main competitors are and what is driving their satisfaction and share among your shared customers. As with the Wallet Allocation Score itself, it is not enough to look only at your own brand. This idea is not new; it's just somewhat foreign in most current discussions about managing customer experience, especially when the focus has been placed on improving a single number.

Barriers

Another common reason that customers use multiple brands is structural barriers that distort demand. In other words, there is some market force that causes people to buy something other than their preferred brand. These market barriers can dramatically influence customers' willingness and ability to devote a greater share of their business to their preferred brand.

In Alex's study of grocery retailers, two prominent structural barriers were found, each affecting different types of stores (see Figure 5.9).

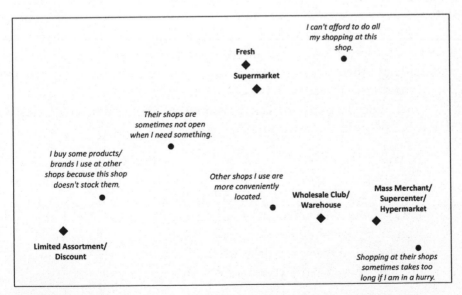

FIGURE 5.9 Perceptual Map Reflecting the Barriers to Using Different Grocery Retailers

The substantially larger footprint of mass merchants and wholesale club/warehouse stores makes it nearly impossible to compete with smaller stores on convenience of location. This issue is not simply a case of store address or number of locations; customers reported that shopping at these types of stores often took "too long." That it takes longer to make one's way through a larger store with "more stuff" is just a physical fact. Conversely, respondents indicated that they could not do "all" their shopping with supermarket- and fresh-format stores because of cost. Although there is almost certainly some room for improvement with clever innovations or targeted pricing strategy, these are realities for which the different players need to prepare.

Often these barriers reflect the power of the distribution channel to limit choice. For example, McDonald's, Burger King, and Wendy's sign exclusive contracts with Coca-Cola or Pepsi to distribute their products—all three currently distribute Coke products in the United States. As a result, loyal Pepsi drinkers dining at these restaurants are forced to substitute a Coke product if they want a soda, or do without entirely.

The most common market barrier is affordability.[15] Although relative price can be a key driver of customers' decisions to use one brand more frequently than another, price also puts many preferred brands out of the usage set entirely. Think of it this way: Most of us would be driving a different car if money were no object.

Another common barrier is that the final buying decision reflects the needs of multiple individuals.[16] In other words, we balance our needs with the needs of others—as a result, we don't purchase the brand we would buy if the decision were entirely our own to make.

Shared decision making is so common in family purchase decisions that it has become a well-worn wedding joke:

> A man was interviewed on his 75th wedding anniversary. "Amazing, 75 years," gushed the interviewer. "What's the secret to such a long, happy marriage?" "It's like this," replied the husband. "The man makes all the big decisions . . . and the woman makes the little decisions." "Does that really work?" asked the interviewer, a little taken aback. "Oh, yes," he said proudly. "Seventy-five years and not one big decision so far."[17]

Although this little tale is obviously designed for a laugh, all of us have at some point compromised on getting exactly what we wanted to meet the needs or desires of others. Overcoming this barrier requires that a brand appeal to multiple decision makers, which requires managers to really understand how consumers choose brands when multiple individuals have input on the final decision.

Market barriers are a factor that managers cannot ignore. The hard reality for managers is that improving customers' experience with the brand will have little impact on share of wallet until the barriers to purchasing the brand are removed. Addressing market barriers are often some of the most difficult tasks.

Demand Evidence

The Wallet Allocation Rule changes the rules of the game. But this is definitely a thinking person's game. Although the rule makes the linkage between customers' perceptions of your brand and the share of spending they allocate to your brand possible, success demands measuring, assessing, and acting on those metrics that are proved to link to customers' buying behaviors.

The Wallet Allocation Rule stands on the fundamental truth that every buying decision that customers make is based on an assessment of the brand vis-à-vis competitive alternatives. Therefore, every customer-related metric that managers use to measure and manage the buying experience needs to reflect the competitive nature of the marketplace.

Seeing the market through this lens makes it clear that no single customer metric is sufficient for guiding a firm. Managers need a full array of metrics and strategic frameworks to help them assess and navigate the ever-changing landscape in which their brands compete.

The metrics presented here can help you identify and leverage real opportunities to improve customers' share of category spending with their brands. This won't make the job of being a manager any easier—you still have to make the hard decisions about what to do to leverage these opportunities. But these metrics will allow you to make smarter decisions—ones that really impact growth!

6

Chapter

Making It Happen

Neither a wise man nor a brave man lies down on the tracks of
history to wait for the train of the future to run over him.[1]
— *Dwight D. Eisenhower, thirty-fourth president*
of the United States

If you want to make enemies, try to change something.[2]
— *Woodrow Wilson, twenty-eighth president of the United States*

Ancient Greek philosopher Heraclitus famously observed, "Nothing
endures but change."[3] We would add, "But unfortunately no one wants
to change."

Companies must change to survive. Nonetheless, organizational
change always meets with resistance.

As a result, change often happens because the pain of the current
situation has become unbearable. For many firms, the gap between the
goals of the chief executive officer (CEO) and the deliverables of the chief
marketing officer (CMO), and marketing in general, has become excru-
ciatingly painful.

This is in large part reflected in the dismal corporate life expectancies
of CMOs. Although consulting firm Spencer Stuart reports that CMO
tenure has steadily increased to an average of 45 months in 2012 from a

low of 23.2 months in 2006,[4] it is still substantially less than half the time a typical CEO spends in that role.[5] For some industries, CMO tenure is far shorter—CMOs in the automotive, communications, health care, and restaurant industries averaged 32 or fewer months in their jobs.

For CMOs to thrive, marketing has to be aligned with the goals of the CEO. And the overriding goal is clear: CEOs are obsessed with the growth of their companies.

The good news is that CEOs recognize that sustainable growth can only be achieved through strong relationships with customers.[6] As marketing is charged with understanding the needs and wants of customers, CMOs should be well positioned to guide their companies' growth strategies.

The bad news is that CMOs have not been able to demonstrate that their efforts have a measurable impact on the share of category spending that customers' give to their brands. As a result, CMOs have far too often not been able to show a positive return on their marketing investments.

In fairness, CMOs could rightly argue that no one could be expected to do this. No system existed that could easily and strongly link customer perceptions about the brands they use to how customers actually allocated their spending.

So although CEOs could lament the current state of marketing in their organizations, the grass wasn't greener on the other side of the fence. A new CMO was likely to fare as well as his or her predecessor.

Of course, that was before the discovery of the Wallet Allocation Rule. Those CMOs who apply the rule will know precisely how customers' divide their spending. More important, they will know what it takes to get more of it!

But that doesn't just happen. It requires a systematic approach for making the Wallet Allocation Rule a road map for driving strategic decisions designed to grow share.

Throughout this book, we have presented the case for the Wallet Allocation Rule and highlighted tools for implementing it in your organizations. Rather than end this book with a cheerleader's call to "Go, Fight, Win!" we instead want to focus on this all too important fact: Without proper execution, good ideas can and often do fail. The Wallet Allocation Rule is no exception.

Next we present the two most basic rules for properly executing the Wallet Allocation Rule. In fact, many readers will likely think they are self-evident. Unfortunately, that is probably the reason they are too often forgotten—with disastrous consequences.

Rule 1: Get the Data Right

To quote a common refrain, "Bad data are worse than no data!"[7] Bad data cost companies between 10 percent and 25 percent of their revenues.[8] All told, the costs to the economy from these errors are easily in the hundreds of billions of dollars, with some estimates topping $3 trillion annually![9]

If bad data were a disease, it would be a plague of biblical proportions. Clearly, no one wants bad data. As a result, most firms institute procedures designed to minimize it. Even so, the fact that the problem is so widespread demonstrates just how difficult it is to ensure the quality of data. Therefore, managers must be ever vigilant in ensuring the quality of data used in their Wallet Allocation Rule analyses.

This raises the question, "What exactly are 'bad' data in the context of the Wallet Allocation Rule?"

Although there are many ways that data can be "bad," the four issues that most commonly contaminate Wallet Allocation Rule analyses are as follows:

1. Inputting erroneous values (i.e., the wrong values are assigned)
2. Measuring the wrong people (i.e., poor sample selection)
3. Measuring the wrong brands (i.e., ignoring competitors)
4. Measuring the wrong things (called "model misspecification")

Inputting Erroneous Values

Inputting erroneous values is primarily a quality control issue. This is the most basic breakdown that can happen. And it happens all the time.

Although the Wallet Allocation Rule is easy to understand, the underlying data necessary to conduct the analysis are more complex than virtually all standard satisfaction or Net Promoter Score studies. It requires tracking satisfaction for all brands your customers use in the category. Because customers vary in the brands that they use, this often means collecting satisfaction information for many different brands.

The satisfaction data then must be converted to ranks (i.e., the brand that a customer gave the highest satisfaction level is assigned a 1, the second highest a 2, and so forth). Moreover, brands receiving the same satisfaction level must be given a rank that represents the average of the ranks they would have occupied had they not been tied (e.g., two brands tied for first would each receive a rank of 1.5 (the average of 1 plus 2 making the next available rank 3).

Although this is conceptually simple, without a good system for making this transformation, it is very easy to make mistakes. And these mistakes always lead to wrong answers.

Measuring the Wrong People

The Wallet Allocation Rule is designed to look at your brand in a market context. In other words, it requires understanding how customers perceive your brand vis-à-vis competitors.

Therefore, managers need to ensure that they are collecting information from the right individuals. It is important to note that "right" can take on many different meanings in terms of who you're surveying. For example, managers may want to target particular segments of customers (e.g., high profit potential, heavy users, etc.). For this discussion, however, we are referring to gathering information from a representative sample of customers.

The first thing a manager must decide on is whether to collect a market representative sample (i.e., a sample of all customers in the category—not just your own customers), or a customer sample (i.e., a sample of customers of your brand only). Both types of samples can work, but each come with pros and cons.

A market sample provides managers with insight into the dynamics of the entire category, not just customers of your business. As such, managers can align their metrics with the market shares of their brands as well as competitors.

Given this, why would any manager choose to use a customer-only sample? In a word, *cost*. Conducting a Wallet Allocation Rule analysis requires collecting information for a valid sample of your brand's customers. When using a market representative sample, that typically means collecting information from a large number of people.

To see how this would be the case, suppose for a moment that you needed information from 500 of your customers to run a valid Wallet Allocation Rule analysis on your brand. If your brand had a 10 percent market share, then you could in theory need to collect data from as many as 5,000 customers (i.e., 500/0.10) to get 500 for your brand.[10] Of course, the number needed is almost always significantly less than the theoretical maximum because customers use multiple brands. But even if you only needed to collect information from half as many people to reach 500 of your customers, that is still a sample of 2,500 people—of which 2,000 are not your customers!

Moreover, the cost of each participant in a market representative survey is almost always significantly higher than for a customer-only sample. That is because firms rarely have contact information for competitors' customers. Therefore, finding these customers and getting them to participate in the survey can be very expensive.

By contrast, a customer-only sample often has very little cost associated with it (particularly if the firm has e-mail contact information for its customers). Because firms know (or should know) their customers, it is much easier to identify and contact a valid sample of customers.

Therefore, managers need to decide if the benefit of a market representative sample is worth the added costs, particularly given that both market and customer-only samples will work with the Wallet Allocation Rule.

Measuring the Wrong Brands

Most managers think about their competitors. In fact, most managers have an idea about who they consider to be their "real" competitors.

Of course, that is only natural—managers tend to think about their businesses all the time. The problem is that customers don't think about competitors the same way that managers do. As a result, one of the biggest mistakes that managers can make is to ignore how customers define the competitors to a brand.

Often, managers have a bias against collecting information for some brands because their firm doesn't consider them to be direct competitors. For example, some traditional grocery retailers prefer to exclude gathering information on Walmart because it is a mass merchandise retailer despite the fact that it accounts for a huge percentage of grocery sales in the United States.

When using the Wallet Allocation Rule, ignoring customer-defined competitors is a very bad idea. The goal of any Wallet Allocation Rule analysis is to understand how and why customers divide their spending among brands in the category. It is the job of management to decide which competitors to target. But without a clear understanding of why customers use each of the brands that they do, there is no way to determine the best approach for improving the share of spending that your customers give to your brand.

Measuring the Wrong Things

By far the most common mistake that managers make when applying the Wallet Allocation Rule relates to uncovering key drivers of and market barriers to increasing share of wallet (discussed in Chapter 5). Here most problems can be classified into one of two categories: (1) not asking important questions and (2) asking too many similar questions.

If an important question is left out, there is no fixing it later in the analysis. Any key driver analysis is limited to the data included. As a result, failure to collect information on an important issue blinds managers to potential opportunities and threats.

That doesn't mean, however, that managers should simply ask lots of questions either. Too many questions has the double whammy of (1) fatiguing customers responding to the survey (thereby significantly decreasing the reliability of their answers) and (2) making it very difficult to tease out what is really going on because many questions tend to be highly correlated to one another.

The right solution to this problem is better questionnaire design. This requires really understanding those aspects of the product and service experience that meaningfully affect customers' decisions to use the brands that they do.

Unfortunately, too often surveys are prescribed by operational areas within a company that are primarily concerned with getting information on either how well they are doing or what they think they should be doing. Sometimes they are designed simply to get "we're awesome" confirmation for internal and external public relations (we refer to these as "smile surveys").

Unfortunately, neither method lends any real insight into what it takes to get customers to allocate more of their business to your brand. This requires speaking with and really listening to customers to uncover the reasons they use the brands that they do.[11]

Rule 2: Set the Right Performance Standards

One of the most important takeaways from the Wallet Allocation Rule is the idea that improved performance must change customers' perceptions of the relative rank of your brand vis-à-vis competing brands. In other words, it's not enough to simply do better—you must do better than your competitors.

A big problem in effectively executing the Wallet Allocation Rule is that managers seldom understand what it really takes (in terms of benefits versus costs) to actually perform better than competitors. As a result, companies rarely identify and focus on the biggest opportunities for growth.

In their *Harvard Business Review* article on creating organic growth, Booz & Company consultants Favaro, Meer, and Sharma present three variables for estimating potential growth opportunities that align well with the Wallet Allocation Rule approach. We believe these should be standard in any company:[12]

1. *Headroom for growth:* "The number of clients and the share of wallet the company doesn't have minus the number of clients and share of wallet it is unlikely to ever have."

2. *Switchers:* "The clients who could be enticed to switch to a provider with a better offering."

3. *Needs-offer gap:* "The difference between the benefits that would cause those clients to switch their business and the benefits their current provider offers."

Using this approach provides managers with a view of the total opportunity. Without a grasp of the big picture, managers often choose conservative, small opportunities that generate high returns on investment (ROIs) but little real profits. Understanding the magnitude of growth opportunities helps keep managers focused on high potential initiatives.

Performance standards then need to be set based on achieving satisfaction levels that result in a shift in rank, thereby causing customers to allocate more of their spending to your brand.

Unfortunately, the current reality is that performance thresholds are almost never based on improving a brand's relative competitive position. Instead, they are most typically based on achieving some arbitrary target. Often the primary motivation for a particular target level is to ensure that it is sufficiently low so that the company reaches the threshold and management receives a bonus.[13]

Of course, that approach almost never results in the type of improvement necessary to make a meaningful difference in the way customers perceive your brand relative to competitors. You either answer the needs-offer gap or you don't. The key to winning has always been the same. It's not how many points you score that matters—it has to be more than your competitor.

The Next Disruption

Shortly after its discovery, the Wallet Allocation Rule received an award for "Disruptive Innovation."[14] Although the recognition has been thrilling, it means little if it does not meaningfully change the way we measure and manage the way customers perceive our brands.

Perhaps the most important contribution of the Wallet Allocation Rule is that it demands that managers move from navel-gazing customer satisfaction and Net Promoter Score surveys to holistic examinations of their brand's performance relative to competitors. Every manager knows that customers make choices based on their perceptions of the competitive landscape. For too long we've ignored that most basic truth in how we measure and manage customer satisfaction and loyalty. So in a very important way, the Wallet Allocation Rule is a testament to the fundamentals of business success.

The Wallet Allocation Rule also helps answer the increasing demand for financial accountability. By measuring opportunities through their impact on customers' share of spending with your brand, managers can gauge the financial outcomes of their investments to improve the customer experience.

Most important, the Wallet Allocation Rule is about making win-win situations. Customers win because companies provide them with what they really need. And because customers have fewer needs to use competitors, companies clearly win by gaining a higher share of their spending.

Of course, that is an old idea made new again through the application of the Wallet Allocation Rule. To quote Peter Drucker one last time, "The aim of marketing is to know and understand the customer so well the product or service fits him and sells itself."[15]

What's Next?

The great end of life is not knowledge but action.[1]
— *Thomas Henry Huxley, distinguished English biologist and*
early advocate of Darwinism

Now that you have read the book, it's time to act on what you've read. Here are some things you can do next to make the Wallet Allocation Rule work for you.

Establish That You Need It

The primary reason to use the Wallet Allocation Rule is that current customer metrics (e.g., satisfaction, Net Promoter Score, etc.) are poor predictors of share of wallet. But please don't simply take our word for it. We strongly recommend you begin by determining the strength of the relationship for yourself. In Chapter 1 (see Figure 1.6) we show an easy way to do this using Microsoft Excel. In our experience, the percentage of variance explained (i.e., R-square) is typically around 1 percent. In other words, 99 percent of customers' share of spending is unexplained by satisfaction or Net Promoter. This is "Oh my God!" bad.

Get Help

We are passionate about helping companies win where it counts—in the spending of their customers. We would be happy to work with you to make the Wallet Allocation Rule an integral part of your customer experience management strategy. To learn more, contact us at info@walletrule.com.

Let's Talk

We love speaking to companies and at events about harnessing the power of the Wallet Allocation Rule in your organization. To have us speak, contact us at speaking@walletrule.com.

Connect with Us

We keep links to many of our research papers up on LinkedIn, and we update our accounts with new research regularly. So connect with us on LinkedIn. *(A couple of rules for our LinkedIn connections: no spamming us or our connections, and no fake LinkedIn profiles.)*

- Tim Keiningham: www.linkedin.com/in/timothykeiningham/
- Lerzan Aksoy: www.linkedin.com/pub/lerzan-aksoy/10/2a4 /450
- Luke Williams: www.linkedin.com/pub/luke-williams/3/631 /a05
- Alex Buoye: www.linkedin.com/pub/alex-buoye/3/376/661

Follow us on Twitter:

- Tim Keiningham: @tkeiningham
- Lerzan Aksoy: @lerzo

Visit www.walletrule.com

For additional resources, advice and insight—and the opportunity to share your own insight—please visit the Web site www.walletrule.com.

Appendix A

Quick Start Guide

To achieve greatness, start where you are, use what you have, do what you can.[1]

—*Arthur Ashe, former American world number 1 ranked professional tennis player and the only black man ever to win the singles title at Wimbledon, the U.S. Open, and the Australian Open*

What Is the Wallet Allocation Rule?

At its core, the Wallet Allocation Rule stipulates that a customer's share of wallet is expected to equal 1 minus the inverse of a customer's rank of the firm/brand relative to the competitors the customer uses.

This simple formula would be all we need if all customers used exactly two firms/brands in a category. But because many customers use one or more than two, we need to weight this based on the number of firms/brands used to make them comparable. This weight equals 2 divided by the number of firms/brands used by a customer.

Mathematically, the formula we use to do this is as follows:

$$Share\ of\ wallet = \left(1 - \frac{rank}{number\ of\ brands + 1}\right) \times \left(\frac{2}{number\ of\ brands}\right)$$

where:

Rank   = the relative position that a customer assigns to a
                        brand in comparison to other brands also used by
                        the customer in the category
Number of brands = the total number of brands used in the category by
                        the customer

To use the Wallet Allocation Rule to predict share of wallet, follow these steps:

1. Establish the firms/brands in a product category that customers use.

2. Ask an overall satisfaction/loyalty question to gauge performance for each firm/brand a customer uses.

3. Assign a performance rank for each firm/brand for each customer (e.g., the highest rated firm/brand based on the overall satisfaction/loyalty question used would be ranked 1, the next highest 2, etc.).

4. Calculate a customer-level Wallet Allocation Score (i.e., the customer's predicted share of wallet) using the rank and number of brands used by the customer.

5. If you want to calculate firm/brand level scores, simply average the Wallet Allocation Scores for each firm's/brand's customers.

The ramifications of the Wallet Allocation Rule are profound. Using this simple formula, managers can easily and strongly link their customer metrics with share of wallet. These findings also point to the need for a new approach for identifying opportunities designed to enhance the customer experience and share of wallet simultaneously.

Using the Wallet Allocation Rule Formula: A Simple Example

Don't let the math worry you. Using the Wallet Allocation Rule is a very simple process.

The chart that follows shows the satisfaction ratings for three financial institutions used by customers John, Jane, Mary, and Tom (1 = completely dissatisfied, 10 = completely satisfied).

	Brand X	Brand Y	Brand Z
JOHN	8	9	10
JANE	7	not used	9
MARY	6	9	8
TOM	7	9	9

FIGURE A.1 Customers' Satisfaction Levels for Brands X, Y, and Z

	Brand X	Brand Y	Brand Z
JOHN	3	2	1
JANE	2	--	1
MARY	3	1	2
TOM	3	1.5	1.5

FIGURE A.2 Relative "Ranked" Satisfaction Levels for Brands X, Y, and Z

The next chart shows the ranks of the three financial institutions based on the satisfaction scores provided by John, Jane, Mary, and Tom. In the case of a tie, as was the case for Tom with Brand Y and Brand Z, assign each a rank for the average of the two places they would have occupied had they not been tied. For example, if two brands are tied for second place, had they not been tied one brand would be in second, the other in third. The average of second and third is 2.5—that is, $(2 + 3) / 2$.

Brands not used are treated as missing and are not assigned a rank, as was the case for Jane with Brand Y.

To arrive at a brand's share of wallet for a given customer, plug the brand's rank and the number of brands used by the customer into the Wallet Allocation Rule formula. For example, calculating John's share for Brand Z would be done as shown in Figure A.3.

Wallet Allocation Rule Strategy

The Wallet Allocation Rule comes with several important strategic implications. First and foremost, managers cannot evaluate their firms without taking competition into account. Although this sounds obvious, the reality is that managers typically evaluate their firm's performance based on customer perceptions of their firm only. As a result, the target objectives used to evaluate and compensate managers are almost never based on

	Brand X	Brand Y	Brand Z
JOHN	3	2	1

$$= \left(1 - \frac{\text{rank}}{\text{number of brands} + 1}\right) \times \frac{2}{\text{number of brands}}$$

$$= \left(1 - \frac{1}{3 + 1}\right) \times \frac{2}{3}$$

$$= (1 - 0.25) \times 0.667$$

$$= 50\%$$

	Brand X	Brand Y	Brand Z
JOHN	16.7%	33.3%	50.0%
JANE	33.3%	0%	66.7%
MARY	16.7%	50.0%	33.3%
TOM	16.7%	41.7%	41.7%

FIGURE A.3 Brand-Level Share of Wallet

changing the perceived rank of the firm vis-à-vis competition. Rather, they are based on achieving a particular score for the firm.

It is rank, however, that actually matters! Every manager knows that it is better to be number one than number two. But the Wallet Allocation Rule makes it very easy for managers to determine the financial implications of that. The difference between first and second is typically quite large. Making that jump can have a tremendous financial impact.

The Wallet Allocation Rule also makes clear that it is not enough to be tied for first place. Parity hurts! There must be a reason for customers to prefer your firm. Otherwise, you evenly divide your customers' share of wallet with your closest competitors.

It is important to remember, however, that although rank is imperative, it isn't the only thing that matters. The number of competitors that your customers use has a significant impact on share of wallet. Being first in a field of three is much better than being first in a field of six. That's because every brand used by a customer gets some percentage of his or her wallet. So the more brands used, the lower the potential share of wallet available for everyone.

These strategic issues have practical implications for how we identify opportunities for improving share of wallet. The traditional approach for identifying opportunities can be thought of as trying to find the answer to the question, "What can we do to make you happier?" Whether it is analyzing customers' open-ended survey responses, or deriving importance through statistical analysis, the focus is virtually always on improving satisfaction with what the firm/brand currently offers.

Performance, however, is relative to competitive alternatives. Improving satisfaction is important because, at some point, increases in satisfaction make a brand more attractive to customers relative to competitors. But that is not enough. Managers also need to understand exactly why customers use each of the brands that they do. Customers have legitimate reasons for using multiple brands in a category. Therefore, efforts designed to improve share of wallet that do not address precisely why your customers also use your competitors are doomed.

One of the most common reasons customers use multiple brands is because they perceive there to be unique benefits associated with each brand they use. For example, credit union and retail bank managers often find that customers use one institution because of lower fees and another because of better Internet banking services. Therefore, reducing fees further for the fee-differentiated institution will not likely prove to be the best opportunity to improve share of deposits, even though low fees are the strongest driver of the institution's customers' satisfaction and loyalty. The competition is being used for another reason.

Another common reason that customers use multiple brands is structural barriers that distort demand. In other words, there is some market force that causes people to buy something other than their preferred brand. The most common of these is a lack of access. The more difficult a brand is to find, the more likely it is to be substituted. So improving customers' experience with the brand will have little impact on share of wallet until the barriers to purchasing it are removed.

Managers can gather this information as part of the Wallet Allocation Rule survey process. This process doesn't have to be complex. It can be as simple as asking customers something like the following:

> *When choosing between brands, what tends to be the deciding factor in choosing one over the other?*
>
> *I choose [Brand 1] when …*
>
> *I choose [Brand 2] when …*

With an understanding of why your customers use your brand as well as competitive brands, you can identify what it really takes to be the first choice of their customers. And because the Wallet Allocation Rule is tied to share of wallet, managers can prioritize their efforts by their potential impact on future revenues.

Identifying Opportunities for Improving Share of Wallet

Traditionally, managers have focused on understanding the "drivers of satisfaction" with their brand. The problem has been that these models tend to ignore competition and focus on changes in the absolute satisfaction score instead of shifts in the relative ranking of the brand vis-à-vis competition. As a result, although satisfaction scores may improve by focusing on the drivers uncovered in these models, share of wallet tends to show very little improvement.

To understand what drives changes in share of wallet, managers need to shift their focus from the "drivers of satisfaction" to the "drivers of rank." As such, managers should work with their research teams to develop statistical models for identifying these drivers.

But managers do not need to wait on complex statistical models to begin using the Wallet Allocation Rule to identify opportunities. That is because at its core, improving your brand's rank means minimizing the reasons your customers have to use competitors. The following is an easy to follow six-step process that managers can use right away:

1. Survey a statistically valid sample of your customers.
2. Use the Wallet Allocation Rule to establish the share of wallet for each competitor used by your customers.
3. Determine how many of your customers use each of the various competitors.
4. Calculate the revenue going to each competitor from your customers.
5. Identify the primary reasons your customers use your competitors.
6. Prioritize opportunities by estimating the costs of addressing the reasons a specific competitor is used by your customers versus the potential financial return. (Don't forget to consider the cumulative impact for issues that span multiple competitors.)

An Example in the Credit Union Industry

Following is a simplified example of some of the information that managers could use from a Wallet Allocation Rule approach to guide their strategy. In this case, the example is set in the credit union market, but the methods are transferable to any industry sector in which customers tend to use multiple brands.

Managers first need to identify where they stand in the minds of their customers. Because the Wallet Allocation Rule uses ranks, it is recommended that credit union managers monitor the percentage of customers who consider the credit union their exclusive first choice (Figure A.4).

The Wallet Allocation Rule also uses the number of competitors used by customers as a key component in the calculation of share (Figure A.5). As a result, managers need to understand how and with whom customers allocate their deposits.

Credit union managers can then use this information to calculate the share of deposits going to their institutions and to their competitors. The advantage of knowing share of wallet (in this case, share of deposits) is that it is very easy to translate it into dollars. To understand which competitors represent the greatest threats and the greatest opportunities,

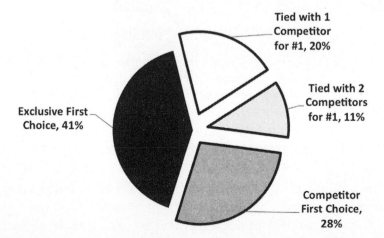

Percentage of My Members Who Consider Credit Union Their First Choice

FIGURE A.4 Percentage of Customers Who Consider the Firm/Brand Their First Choice

Percent of Your Credit Union Members Holding Deposits with Other Financial Institutions

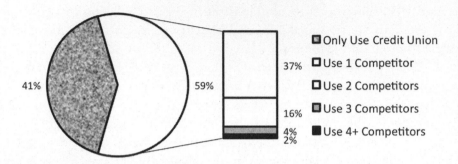

FIGURE A.5 Percentage of a Firm's Customers Using Competitors

Total Deposits Going to Competition from My Members ($ Million)

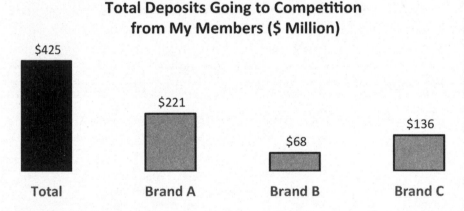

FIGURE A.6 Money Going to Competitors from Your Brand's Customers

managers need to establish how much money their customers are giving their competitors (Figure A.6).

The next step is to identify exactly what drives first choice not only for your credit union but also for your competitors (Figure A.7). Customers have a logical reason for using each institution that they do. Winning back share requires minimizing the reasons customers have for using the competition.

In the case of this example, a low fee structure largely drives customers to choose the credit union as their first choice. Competitors, however, are competing on different aspects of coverage: Internet

Primary Reason My Members Use My Credit Union and the Competition

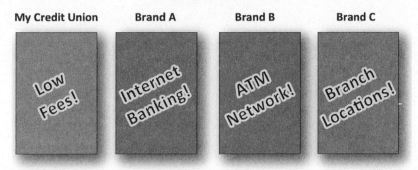

FIGURE A.7 Primary Reasons Your Customers Use the Competition

banking, ATM network, and branch locations. Examining first choice drivers through this lens of varied coverage allows managers to determine which competitors are easier and which are more difficult to address in the short term. In the case of this example, competing against Brand C will be more difficult in the short term because it requires that credit unions address the convenience of branch locations.

Knowing what drives customers to use the competition allows managers to focus on their greatest near-term opportunities—in this case either Internet banking or ATM network. Brand A, however, is doing a much better job of capturing customers' share of deposits. As a result, managers should first consider the feasibility of addressing Brand A's point of competitive advantage.

Conclusion

The key to growth is improved share of wallet. Although most managers instinctively know this to be true, the problem has always been how to do it. The Wallet Allocation Rule now makes it possible to understand what it really takes to be number one.

Frequently Asked Questions

There are naive questions, tedious questions, ill-phrased questions, questions put after inadequate self-criticism. But every question is a cry to understand the world. There is no such thing as a dumb question.[1]

— *Carl Sagan, American astronomer, astrophysicist,
cosmologist, and author*

When Is It Appropriate to Use the Wallet Allocation Rule?

The Wallet Allocation Rule focuses on improving the share of wallet of a brand's customers. Therefore, it is most relevant in situations in which a large percentage of a brand's customers also use a competing brand. Generally speaking, a category in which at least 40 percent of customers are "polygamous" (i.e., multibrand users) qualifies as a so-called repertoire market in which the Wallet Allocation Rule is applicable. In situations in which "hyperpolygamy" (i.e., using many brands) is common, an even larger number of monogamous customers can work. In terms of minimum average usage set size, a good rule of thumb is 1.4.[2]

For subscription (e.g., contractual services) or monogamous markets, the general concepts of the Wallet Allocation Rule can be applied to the list of brands a customer would consider using. This provides a context for the evaluation of the brand currently used versus perceptions of its competitors, which can be the basis for a measure of brand equity. To measure the impact of specific features, pricing considerations, and so on, discrete choice modeling[3] is a useful addendum to this kind of analysis.

Does the Wallet Allocation Rule Work with All Satisfaction Metrics?

That is, does the wallet allocation rule work with overall satisfaction (i.e., consumers' general satisfaction with the firm or brand, also known as cumulative or summary satisfaction), transaction-specific satisfaction (e.g. consumers' satisfaction with a specific encounter involving the firm or brand), or both overall and transaction-specific satisfaction?

The Wallet Allocation Rule is best applied to satisfaction metrics that capture a holistic evaluation of customers' relationships with the brand. We know from previous research that summary satisfaction is largely a function of transactional satisfaction,[4] but this relationship is not easily measured in this way because it requires multiple responses from the same customers over time. Thus, a relationship study provides a more efficient way to analyze broader issues.

Even more important, however, is that these evaluations are put in the context of customers' perceptions of the other brands they use. Generally speaking, it is not practical to collect this type of information in a survey focused on a single transaction. Rather, the purpose of transactional surveys is to identify service quality issues so that managers can address them quickly. Moreover, although quality control issues are important to correct, most of them are not likely to be the key dimensions of the customer experience that determine where customers will shop.

The ideal way to use the Wallet Allocation Rule in conjunction with transaction-specific surveys is to first conduct a relationship study capturing competitive evaluations, identify those dimensions of the customer experience that most influence customers' decisions about where to shop (using the Wallet Allocation Rule process), and then ensure that these metrics are being tracked in the transaction-specific survey along with the more operational service quality measures that are characteristic of this type of survey.

Is There a Preferred Metric We Should Use to Determine a Brand's Rank?

The Wallet Allocation Rule appears to work well with any of the most commonly used metrics (e.g., satisfaction, recommend intention, purchase intention, Net Promoter Score classifications: promoter, passive, and detractor, etc.). Brand rankings, however, must be made at the customer level.

We do not advocate asking customers explicitly to assign ranks because they will tend to force brands into specific rank levels even when they see no meaningful difference in some brands. Therefore, we need to use a system that easily allows for ties. It is much easier for customers responding to a survey to have ties when using ratings of commonly used satisfaction and loyalty metrics.

For the ratings themselves, some researchers prefer multi-item indices to single-item measures, and these types of multidimensional metrics are often more reliable, valid, and predictive than single-item measures. Within the context of the Wallet Allocation Rule, however, they may create a false sense of precision. For example, one might use a simple average of five 10-point scales as the basis of the ranking instead of a single question. If a respondent rated one brand 9-9-8-10-9 and another brand 9-8-8-10-9, the two brands' averaged scores would be 9 versus 8.8, respectively. If we convert these scores into ranks, the brand with the score of 9 will be ranked ahead of the brand with the 8.8, but it is reasonable to question whether that 0.2 difference is meaningful. In some cases, it may be useful to round the scores from multi-item indices to prevent too much discrimination while still taking advantage of the benefits of using multi-item constructs.

However, because single-item measures have shown to be sufficient in our research and development and have practical benefits (e.g., shorter surveys, less respondent fatigue—remember, respondents will be asked to rate each brand in the usage set, so multiple items in the index will be asked multiple times), we generally recommend sticking with single-item measures as the basis of the rankings.

In terms of scale points, as a default, we recommend 10-point scales, although anything between 7 and 11 points should provide sufficient discrimination.[5] In the case of rounding the scores from multi-item scales, we recommend discretizing to a similar number of points. The Wallet Allocation Rule will still work with 5-point or even 3-point scales, but differentiation of respondents' evaluations may be insufficient resulting in an excessive number of ties.

How Do I Ensure That All Relevant Competitors Are Ranked?

The customer determines the competitors that he or she uses in a given period. To avoid too narrowly defining the category, we suggest asking survey respondents to list all brands used to meet the needs that the category is designed to fulfill (e.g., "all of your grocery shopping needs," etc.). As a rule of thumb, we recommend that the number of brands rated account for at least 90 percent of the respondent's usage for the period in question.[6]

What Metrics Should Be on My "Dashboard" Related to the Wallet Allocation Rule?

There are numerous managerially relevant metrics related to the Wallet Allocation Rule, but here are the three we believe are imperative to track:

1. *Percent first choice*: the percentage of your customers that rank your brand first choice (ties for first choice excluded). First choice is a metric that all employees can understand and rally behind. More important, it has strong impact on share of wallet. This is the metric that should be promoted within the organization.

2. *Average number of brands used*: the average number of firms/brands used in the category by your customers. The Wallet Allocation Rule also makes clear that the number of brands used in the category by a customer has a strong impact on share of wallet. As a result, managers need to understand how and with whom customers allocate their category spending.

3. *Share of wallet:* the average share of wallet that your customers give to your brand. Share of wallet is arguably the most important demonstration of customers' loyalty to your brand.

Why Does the Wallet Allocation Rule Work?

It is intuitive that the amount a customer spends on a brand would be a function of how he or she ranked that brand vis-à-vis other competitors that he or she also used. We would naturally expect the preferred choice to be used more than the next best choice. We would also expect that the more brands used, the lower the share of wallet available for a given rank.

The core of the Wallet Allocation Rule, however, goes beyond intuition—it is a scientific law. Zipf's law states that the frequency of occurrence of some event is inversely proportional to its rank. Many types of data studied in the physical and social sciences have been shown to be inversely proportional to rank: corporation sizes, Internet usage, world income distribution, frequency of any word in a language, and so on. Researchers have shown that market shares and even share of wallet follow Zipf's law.

The Wallet Allocation Rule is clearly an example of Zipf's law, but using the rule differs significantly from using the Zipf distribution, which is typically associated with this law.

Using the Zipf distribution is mathematically complex, computationally intensive, and requires a lot of data. It requires determining the value of an exponent to fit the correct distribution. Specifically, managers must input both rank and share of wallet data into a database. They then need to computationally back-solve the formula to determine the appropriate value(s) of the exponent.

The Wallet Allocation Rule avoids the complexity associated with the Zipf distribution—managers only need to know the rank and number of brands used.

Will Relative Net Promoter Score Work?

Many firms track what is referred to as relative Net Promoter Score (NPS). Because the Wallet Allocation Rule is based on relative satisfaction (or

NPS classifications), managers using relative NPS ask "Do I really need to do anything differently?" If the goal is to link NPS to share of wallet, then the short answer is yes. The first thing to note is that NPS is a firm-level metric, not a customer-level metric. Therefore, relative NPS typically means that the focal firm is comparatively better or worse than other firms in the category based on differences in NPS levels.

Unfortunately, firm-level (aggregate-level) metrics won't work if the goal is improved share of wallet. This analysis must be done at the customer level.

There are actually statistical rules for when you are allowed to aggregate data.[7] A simple rule of thumb is that you are never allowed to aggregate data when the relationship between the variable you are tracking and the outcome variable is very weak. Without going into too much detail as to why, the "averages" you come up with by aggregating the data cancel out the extremes (think people above and below the mean). As a result, you end up with what is called an ecological fallacy—simplistically, you mistakenly think you understand individuals within the group.

Therefore, you must first get the customer-level relationship between your metric of choice (e.g., satisfaction, recommend intention, Net Promoter Score classifications: promoter, passive, or detractor) to link strongly to share of wallet *before* you can aggregate the data. This is best done by converting these measures to relative ranks. Although you can use any of the previously listed metrics to derive relative rank—and thereby link to share of wallet—you cannot simply use the firm-level metric (relative or absolute level). It will almost always result in getting the wrong answer about what is driving customers' share of category spending.

Isn't Share of Wallet Just a Function of a Brand's Reach (i.e., Penetration)?

There is an observable phenomenon known as double jeopardy, wherein brands with the greatest number of customers also tend to have higher purchase frequencies among those customers. And of course, more purchases equals greater share of wallet. So, the argument goes, brands win (or lose) twice when they extend (or lessen) their reach—they get more customers and their average purchase frequency goes up. Proponents of this model argue that it is therefore impossible to increase share of wallet without increasing a brand's penetration.

Without question, double jeopardy is real. Moreover, penetration is important to market share growth.

The Dirichlet model (the mathematical model used to describe double jeopardy), however, is an aggregate- (or brand-) level model, and as we have presented in this book, share of wallet is an individual-level measure. The Dirichlet model explains a great deal of the variation in average share of wallet among brands, but it explains almost none of the variation in share of wallet among customers of those brands. In our own research, we have used multilevel modeling procedures to estimate the percent of variance in share of wallet that can be explained by the brands that individuals use. In short, only about 20 percent to 30 percent of the variation in share of wallet can be explained by looking "between brands." The remaining 70 percent to 80 percent of variation in share of wallet occurs "within brands." In other words, there is a lot more variation between Customer A, Customer B, and Customer C of Brand X than there is between Brand X and Brand Y. The Wallet Allocation Rule helps you to understand that 70 percent to 80 percent and how to improve your brand's share using a bottom-up rather than top-down approach.

Furthermore, even when looking specifically at the brand level, our research shows that brand-level models that incorporate an aggregate indicator of *relative* satisfaction (in the case of our research, percent first choice) explain much more variance in *average* share of wallet than models that focus only on penetration.[8]

For sure, double jeopardy is real, and may, in fact, help us to understand the limits to growth that can be expected using a share of wallet strategy. But we also don't want to mistake correlation for causation. Individual consumers do not decide how much to use various brands based on brand presence alone.

Visit www.walletrule.com

We will keep testing the Wallet Allocation Rule to find its limits and to advance best practices. And we will continue to subject our ideas and findings to the scrutiny of the scientific community so that managers can have confidence that what we report is vetted and robust. Therefore, we encourage you to visit the Web site www.walletrule.com to access the latest Wallet Allocation Rule research and resources.

Acknowledgments

A little help from my friends[1]
> —*John Lennon and Paul McCartney, founding members*
> *of The Beatles*

Principal Contributors

Although this book has four authors listed on the cover, it would not have been nearly as compelling without the contributions of many of our Ipsos Loyalty colleagues from around the world who apply the Wallet Allocation Rule day in and day out in their work. Their contributions to the examples we present in Chapter 3 tangibly demonstrate the robustness of the Wallet Allocation Rule across countries, cultures, and industries.

Therefore, we want to thank and acknowledge the contributions to this book from the following individuals who formed the core research team behind these cases.

Charles Adriaenssens

Charles Adriaenssens is head of financial services for Ipsos Loyalty in the UK. Charles has significant experience in conducting research in the retail financial services marketplace, having spent more than 20 years working exclusively in the sector. At Ipsos, he leads the overall financial services business.

Charles has significant experience in running transactional and relational loyalty programs in the retail financial services sector, and he recently presented at the Market Research Society conference on how customer experience data can be used to drive business change.

Charles is also an expert in joining multiple data sources to tell a "story," incorporating primary and secondary research as well as internal and third-party–"owned" customer data. Among his recent publications is a paper published by CFEB (Consumer Financial Education Body), "Transforming financial behaviour," which investigated how interventions can be used to drive positive behavior change among financial consumers.

Jon Atkin

Jon Atkin is a vice president at Ipsos Loyalty, United States. He leads a number of important relationships in the retail industry. His experience is in designing, managing, and executing a number of large-scale customer experience, enterprise feedback management, and employee engagement programs. Jon's role focuses on helping clients to use research results to drive strategic decision making and organizational change, embedding customer research into day-to-day business decisions of managers at all levels of the organization.

Jon received a bachelor of science (with honors) in psychology from the University of Wales Institute, Cardiff.

John Carroll III

John Carroll III is the global head of clients for Ipsos Loyalty. In this capacity, John advises senior executives across industry sectors in the areas of customer experience innovation, customer strategy development, and customer loyalty improvement. In addition to serving clients, John regularly speaks at major conferences (Beijing, Delhi, Dubai, London, New York, Santiago, and Singapore in 2012–2014), publishes on thought leadership, and is interviewed by the media for expert guidance matters relating to customer experience, satisfaction, and loyalty. He is a specialist in the areas of enterprise feedback management (EFM); social, local, and mobile customer experience; and brand management platforms and systems. John has deployed wallet allocation tools and techniques for numerous clients and is an expert in helping business executives devise competitive customer experience and business strategies based on wallet allocation thinking.

Currently based in Chicago, John is a dual national of the United States and Ireland, and has lived and worked in Europe, Asia, and Africa for a total of over 10 years. Prior to Ipsos, John gained a broad range of experiences helping organizations resolve critical strategic issues while working at McKinsey & Company and Deloitte. John earned an MBA with distinction from the Kellogg School of Management at Northwestern University and a bachelor of science in foreign service from Georgetown University with certificates in international business diplomacy and African studies. He continues to act as an admissions interviewer for both schools.

Pakee Charoenchanaporn

Pakee Charoenchanaporn is a research director at Ipsos Loyalty in Thailand. He manages both Thai and international business-to-business and business-to-consumer research projects across a variety of business sectors. He oversees all aspects of project management, including business development, study design, program management, report writing, and action planning. Before joining Ipsos, Pakee began his career in marketing working with Thai Samsung Electronics and Acorn Marketing.

Pakee received a bachelor of business administration (majoring in international business management) from Assumption University (Thailand), and a master's of commerce in marketing from the University of Sydney (Australia).

Kelvin Chen

Kelvin Chen is managing director of Ipsos Loyalty in China. He has worked for almost two decades in market research, and has experience across a broad range of research specialisms: advertising, brand, satisfaction and loyalty, consumer attitude and usage, and new product introduction. His current work concentrates on the needs of financial services, telecommunications, and consumer durables industries. As such, he works with many of the leading companies in China.

Miranda Cheung

Miranda Cheung is chief executive officer (CEO) of Ipsos Singapore and Malaysia offices. Miranda has led the Singapore office for Ipsos (formerly Synovate) since 2005. Under her leadership, Ipsos Singapore is one of the leading market research agencies today. Given her success, in 2014, Miranda also took over the leadership of Ipsos Malaysia.

Miranda began her career in market research over 20 years ago. In that time, she has chalked up experience across a diverse range of industries, including finance, telecommunications, technology, tourism, retail, and media.

She plays a vital role in the success of many large-scale multimarket research studies for global corporations managed out of Singapore.

Nancy Costopoulos

Nancy Costopoulos is senior vice president of Ipsos Loyalty in the United States, responsible for management of the retail practice. In this role, she oversees all customer and employee research for a broad range of retailers, focused on satisfaction, loyalty, and customer experience management.

Nancy has spent more than 25 years in marketing research across a number of specializations but is most passionate about her loyalty expertise in guiding customer-centric strategies for her clients. Nancy is a graduate of Rutgers University with a dual degree in economics and psychology.

Jean-Francois Damais

Jean-Francois Damais is deputy managing director of global client solutions for Ipsos Loyalty. As a global director, Jean-Francois has acquired extensive experience in understanding and measuring service brands and customer relationships across a wide range of sectors and geographies. Over the past few years he has contributed to development and global rollout of several innovative solutions in the loyalty area, and has successfully applied wallet allocation approaches to provide strategic input and guidance to clients. He is also an accomplished trainer and has an all-round knowledge of Loyalty issues ranging from strategic to tactical. He heads an international team specialized in the modeling of both structured and unstructured data. Jean-Francois is a French national currently working and living in the UK.

Diego de la Barra

Diego is a sociologist, customer loyalty researcher, and director of new business development at Ipsos Loyalty Chile. Diego has a strong background in quantitative research and statistics. These skills have allowed him to work as project manager for a number of large Chilean and international clients across a variety of industries. As a result, his work largely focuses on formulating appropriate methodological approaches to clients' unique needs, and on managing the development of new business opportunities.

Heiko Dees

Heiko Dees joined Ipsos Germany in 2010 and is leading a team of researchers for customer experience and customer loyalty programs in the telecommunications, insurance, financial services, and energy sectors. A large part of his work covers challenges posed by business-to-business research.

Prior to joining Ipsos, his career included consulting work, market research in academic settings, and sales consultancy for Hewlett-Packard. He holds a doctorate in business administration from Technical University of Braunschweig, Germany. His doctoral thesis focused on international marketing in e-commerce.

İlkim Erkan

İlkim Erkan is an econometrician, statistician, and a researcher for Ipsos Loyalty in Turkey. She has been engaged in marketing research for almost a decade working with global and local research companies in Turkey. She joined Ipsos in 2012 as a group leader responsible for business-to-business and business-to-consumer customer loyalty and employee engagement research across a wide variety of industry sectors (e.g., energy, tourism, transportation, digital platforms, construction, retail, consumer electronics, etc.).

İlkim is a graduate of Marmara Üniversitesi with a degree in econometrics.

Amir Fahim

Amir Fahim is the managing director of Ipsos Kuwait. In this role, he oversees all research projects for Ipsos in Kuwait.

Amir has more than 20 years of experience in market research and has wide experience and expertise in the financial services and telecommunications sectors. Prior to joining Ipsos, he held various senior research roles with Americana, KPMG, PARC, and Global Capital Group, where he managed various local and multinational market research accounts.

Amir holds a bachelor degree in business administration from Ain Shams University in Cairo, as well as a Chartered Institute of Marketing diploma from the Institute in the UK.

Nicolás Fritis Cofré

Nicolás Fritis Cofré is managing director of Ipsos Loyalty in Chile. As head of this unit, Nicolás manages the largest loyalty, satisfaction and customer experience tracking programs conducted in Chile with leading local and global brands. Nicolás experience is centered on retail, telecommunications, and banking.

Prior to heading the loyalty division, Nicolás was managing director of Ipsos ASI. Before arriving to Ipsos, he worked at Young & Rubicam as Latin America director of the BrandAsset Valuator™ (BAV), where he focused his experience on brands and marketing.

Nicolás is a graduate of the Universidad de Chile with a degree in civil engineering and also holds an MBA from the same university.

Casandra Fueyo

Casandra Fueyo is account director at Ipsos Loyalty Mexico. She is passionate about helping her clients succeed through better, actionable customer insights. Her experience across a wide range of research techniques and specializations (e.g., brand management, advertising, satisfaction and loyalty, etc.) allow her to address clients' unique needs through research. As a result, Casandra works with most of the leading financial services companies in Mexico.

Casandra is a graduate of the Instituto Tecnológico y de Estudios Superiores de Monterrey (ITESM) with a degree in business administration.

Thomas Gallagher

Tom Gallagher is a vice president at Ipsos Loyalty in the United States. He is a recognized expert in brand loyalty research and performance tracking, including the development of programs for a wide range of industry leaders including Procter & Gamble, Johnson & Johnson, McDonald's,

MasterCard, MTV Networks, and the National Football League (NFL).

Tom has extensive experience in the application of the Wallet Allocation Rule system, with particular emphasis in the financial services industry.

Prior to joining Ipsos Loyalty in 2012, Tom served as president of Gallagher-Lee Research where he specialized in conducting customer loyalty, brand equity, and market tracking research for leading U.S. corporations in health care, consumer products, financial services, and other industries.

His previous research industry experience also includes 10 years at the RCL Division of NFO Worldwide where he developed large-scale brand equity studies, and a broad range of global customer and brand tracking programs.

Tom earned a bachelor of science degree in marketing and general management from Lehigh University. He is also a member of the American Marketing Association and the Pharmaceutical Marketing Research Group (PMRG).

Sidar Gedik

Sidar Gedik is the managing director of Ipsos Loyalty in Turkey. In this role, he oversees all satisfaction and loyalty research for Ipsos in Turkey. He works with a variety of business stakeholders (e.g., employees, customers, dealers, suppliers, etc.) across numerous industry sectors (e.g., automotive, banking, telecommunications, etc.).

Sidar has worked in the research industry for more than 15 years. He began his career working in retail store space optimization. Following this, he worked as a competition and feasibility analyst for one of the biggest Internet service providers in Turkey.

Since 2001 Sidar has worked for Ipsos KMG. He is a member of Ipsos KMG's executive committee, and a member of Ipsos Loyalty's global management board. He is also a member of the Turkish Researchers Association.

Sidar earned a bachelor's degree in industrial engineering from Istanbul Technical University and a master's degree from the University of Marmara.

Alexandre Guérin

Alexandre Guérin is president of Ipsos Loyalty in the United States. Prior to this position, he was managing director of Ipsos Loyalty in France.

As head of Ipsos Loyalty in the United States, Alexandre oversees all studies on management of customer relations and employee relations, including the measurement and management of satisfaction, loyalty, and commitment, as well as loyalty program optimization, action planning, and return on investment measurement. His passion is bridging research and technology to gain the best possible insights from research.

Prior to joining Ipsos, Alexandre began his career in fast-moving consumer goods (FMCG) marketing before spending six years as a consultant with AT Kearney specializing in marketing and management change assignments across Europe.

Alexandre is a graduate of Hautes études commerciales de Paris (HEC School of Management in Paris).

Martin Hellich

Martin Hellich is the managing director of Ipsos Loyalty in Germany. He is in charge of all stakeholder experience and management as well as performance and quality studies. Martin believes that when research drives change in organizations, it results in a positive return on investment (ROI).

Prior to joining Ipsos Loyalty, Martin worked at Bearing Point, TNS Infratest, and Ipsos Marketing.

Martin is a graduate of the economics program at the University of Freiburg.

Hector Jaso Guerrero

Hector Jaso Guerrero is managing director of Ipsos Loyalty in Brazil. In this capacity, Hector oversees all loyalty-related business (e.g., satisfaction and loyalty, customer experience management, quality measurement, etc.) conducted in the region. Prior to heading the loyalty division in Brazil, Hector was managing director of Ipsos Loyalty in Mexico.

Hector has worked in the market research industry for over 15 years. He has extensive experience across many different industry sectors, including fast-moving consumer goods (FMCG), technology, telecommunications, finance, and automotives.

Hector is a graduate of the Instituto Tecnológico Autónomo de México (ITAM) with a degree in actuarial science.

Emmanuelle Jégo

Emmanuelle Jégo is scientific director for Ipsos Loyalty in France. In that role, she oversees data management and statistical analysis for the division.

Emmanuelle has worked in the research industry for more than 15 years, which include over 13 years working in various roles within Ipsos. This broad experience has provided her with a unique skill set, thereby enabling her to select the right approach for addressing a specific problem.

Emmanuelle's work focuses on data fusion and customer relationship management (CRM) analytics to provide clients with enhanced insights from their customer satisfaction and loyalty programs. She is passionate about applying new technologies (e.g., text and Web analytics) to glean new, managerially relevant insights.

Amr Kais

Dr. Amr Kais is the managing director of Ipsos Egypt. He is an experienced practitioner in the fields of marketing and management. His extensive experience in these fields has been acquired through various teaching assignments, consulting practices, and employment with international as well as local conglomerates. Dr. Kais's background comprises a thorough blend of academic expertise and hands-on experience in marketing and management.

Dr. Kais is presently a participating faculty member at the American University in Cairo (undergraduate curriculum, graduate curriculum, Chartered Institute of Marketing, and International Advertising Association [IAA] diploma), Misr International University, and a designated lecturer at various institutions, including the University of Cambridge (Cambridge International Examinations), and the World Bank Institute.

Dr. Kais is a certified management consultant by the Institute of Management Consultancy (IMC) and a certified coach by the Learning Circle on Peter Senge's "team learning labs." His consulting experience is specialized in marketing and management and covers a wide spectrum of industries including automotives, pharmaceuticals, real estate, communications, and advertising fast-moving consumer goods (FMCGs), among others.

Dr. Kais received his DBA from the Maastricht School of Management, Netherlands, and holds the M. Phil. from the same university. Dr. Kais obtained his MBA from the American University in Cairo and his bachelor's degree (marketing and international business specialization) from Cairo University.

Ray Kong

Ray Kong is an experienced marketing professional with 25 years of experience in both consulting and at the executive level of major Canadian financial institutions. As executive vice president with Ipsos, he leads

the Ipsos Canada Loyalty practice and works in the financial services sector in customer experience, brand development and measurement, and operational improvement and strategy projects. Ray is a member of the Ipsos Global Financial Services Centre of Excellence with the role to act as a hub coordinating Ipsos work in financial services around the world and to bring the best of Ipsos work to local clients. He has been an adjunct professor of marketing at York University—a role that regularly tests his ability to stay abreast of emerging and evolving social networking and other Web utilities. A published academic author, he speaks extensively on consumer trends, marketing trends, and best practices of organizations in customer experience, ethnic marketing, and loyalty.

Anna Koren

Anna is a market research professional with almost a decade of experience in the customer satisfaction and loyalty research industry.

Since joining Ipsos Loyalty, Anna has worked with numerous Fortune 500 companies to help them uncover what drives consumer attitudes and behaviors. Her primary areas of expertise include measuring customer loyalty, performance tracking, competitive landscape analysis, new product development, questionnaire design, consumer panels, and emerging customer segments.

At Ipsos Loyalty, Anna is responsible for designing and executing large-scale tracking studies and custom research initiatives, both domestic and global, across diverse industry sectors. She is passionate about helping clients uncover new insights and transforming research findings into meaningful strategy.

Anna holds bachelor degrees from New York University in psychology and biology.

Rentia Krämer

Rentia Krämer is the director of Ipsos Loyalty in South Africa. She has more than 20 years of experience in the market research industry. At Ipsos she is mainly responsible for business strategy, implementation, and growth, as well as client relationship development.

Prior to joining Ipsos, she worked for leading research and strategic planning agencies. She also spent time working on the client side, gaining valuable experience and insight as a research user. She has worked on and managed business-to-consumer and business-to-business studies for a large number of blue chip companies, mainly in the consumer products, financial, IT, telecommunications, and automotive industries. She has a broad range of experience in customer satisfaction and trade marketing research, product testing, brand and communications testing and tracking, and retail auditing.

Rentia holds a master's degree in business leadership from the Graduate School of Business Leadership of the University of South Africa. In addition, she holds a bachelor of arts degree and a certificate in marketing from the University of the Witwatersrand. She is a full member and accredited researcher of the Southern African Market Research Association.

Helen Lee

Helen Lee is managing director of Ipsos in China. She is a well-known expert in the market research industry, with more than 20 years of extensive experience.

Helen has a strong sense of ownership and entrepreneurship, and a passion for innovation. This was honed by her experience as the cofounder of a successful Chinese market research firm, which was acquired by Ipsos in 2000.

Helen also serves as the president of Ipsos Loyalty in China. In that role, she has been overseeing the analysis and strategic recommendations for a large number of international and local clients from a wide range of industries.

Helen received an MBA degree from Fudan University in 2003. She is currently attending the executive MBA (EMBA) course at the China Europe International Business School.

Rafael Lindemeyer

Rafael Lindemeyer is account director at Ipsos Loyalty in Brazil. Rafael is also responsible for the mystery shopping practice within Brazil. Rafael has worked for almost two decades in market research with a great deal of that experience devoted to the retail sector. Prior to joining Ipsos, his career included work in market research with KLM Estatística e Pesquisa, Walmart Brazil, and Kantar Worldpanel. Rafael is a graduate of the Universidade Federal do Rio Grande do Sul in Brazil with a degree in statistics.

Sergio Litvac

Sergio Litvac is director of Ipsos Loyalty in Brazil. He has worked for more than two decades in market research and has experience across a broad range of research specializations, including branding and communications, customer satisfaction, employee engagement, consumer attitude and usage, and product and concept tests. His current work concentrates on satisfaction and loyalty in the financial services industry. He is a member of the financial services steering group in Ipsos. In addition, Sergio leads a team of researchers who work with other industries. As such, he works with many of the leading companies in Brazil.

Ben Llewellyn

Ben Llewellyn is director of enterprise feedback management (EFM) for Ipsos Loyalty. In this role, Ben oversees Ipsos EFM solutions on a global level. He advises clients on the best means of capturing real-time customer feedback, disseminating the information throughout the organization, and helping clients take concrete actions to improve their customers' experience at an individual level.

Originally from the UK, Ben is based in Kuala Lumpur, Malaysia. Prior to his current role, Ben was managing director of Synovate Malaysia. Having spent more than 10 years working in Malaysia and throughout Asia Pacific, Ben has significant exposure to the vast diversity of the region. As a result, Ben is able to bring a truly global perspective when advising clients on how to build strategies that revolve around customer experiences.

Nicholas Lygo-Baker

Nick Lygo-Baker is the head of mystery shopping EMEA (Europe, the Middle East, and Africa) and enterprise feedback management (EFM) implementation and retail for Ipsos Loyalty UK. Nick joined Ipsos MORI in 2013 with over 14 years of experience in businesses performance improvement through customer experience measurement.

A retail and hospitality specialist, Nick has helped businesses through innovating and applying customer feedback solutions across digital, mobile, SMS (short message service), and IVR (interactive voice response) channels to empower employees to positively respond to feedback and improve their customers' experiences.

Nick is a millennial graduate of Bournemouth University with an honours degree in retail management.

Arun Menon

Arun Menon is head of Ipsos Loyalty in Malaysia. Arun joined Ipsos in 2007. Prior to his current role, he was head of quantitative research, Ipsos Kuwait, and regional champion for financial sector services, Ipsos Loyalty MENAP (Middle East, North Africa, Afghanistan, and Pakistan).

He is passionate about helping to make organizations customer centric and driving change through research insights. During the last decade, Arun has been engaging clients across multiple sectors from Asia, Middle East, and Africa.

He holds a bachelor of engineering degree from the University of Calicut and an MBA in marketing and operations from the Amrita School of Business.

Elie Nawar

Elie Nawar is managing director for Ipsos Qatar and Bahrain. In this role, he oversees all research for these two countries.

Elie is an experienced manager who has spent more than 15 years in the market research industry. He has worked on projects spanning all divisions within Ipsos (e.g., loyalty, advertising, public relations, media, etc.). As a result, he has managed the coordination of complex projects that cross research types and geographic locations.

Elie graduated from Lebanese University with a bachelor's degree in advertising and public relations.

Melanie Ng

Melanie specializes in research-based consultancy and leads our loyalty research team in Singapore. Her extensive experience in managing customer experience and loyalty programs is instrumental in guiding her clients across industries through marketing research.

Over her past 20 years of experience, Melanie has led multiple local, regional, and global loyalty programs for many of the world's most prominent brands.

Her passion to bring about insights is clearly demonstrated through the actionable results that she delivers to drive business changes and improvements.

Manjiri Patwardhan

Manjiri Patwardhan is a vice president with Ipsos Loyalty where she leads large-scale loyalty research programs in the travel and hospitality sector. In her extensive experience with client management, loyalty research, and corporate communications, Manjiri has successfully led customer experience research programs for Fortune 500 companies that guide strategic goal setting, product engineering, and customer loyalty analytics.

Manjiri received an MBA in marketing intelligence and management consulting from the University of Connecticut and an undergraduate degree in statistics, mathematics, and physics from the University of Pune, India.

Suraya Randawa

Suraya Randawa is head of financial services at Ipsos Loyalty UK. She has worked across the financial services sector in the UK, across EMEA (Europe, the Middle East, and Africa) and at a global level leading customer satisfaction and loyalty programs for global financial providers. Along with working with clients in retail banking and insurance to help engage customers and deliver business change, Suraya is passionate about cards and emerging payments.

Suraya holds an MPhil in international relations from the University of Cambridge and an MA in economics and international relations from the University of St. Andrews.

Niall Rae

Niall Rae is managing director of Ipsos Loyalty in the UK. Prior to this position, he managed the technology research team at GfK.

As head of Ipsos Loyalty in the UK, Niall manages one of the largest loyalty teams in the Ipsos network covering all key capabilities around customer management and employee engagement including customer journey mapping, stakeholder engagement, relationship and transactional feedback management, activation workshops, and big data analytics. His passion is bringing new technologies and techniques to aid in client understanding of their customers and employees with recent focuses on real-time customer feedback management and the use of neuroscience in getting under the surface of customer journeys.

Niall is a graduate of the London Guildhall University.

Leonardo Rivera

Leonardo Rivera is managing director of Ipsos Loyalty Mexico. With more than 10 years of experience in the market research industry, his key focus has always been customer experience, satisfaction, and loyalty measurement and management in the automotive and financial sectors.

Leonardo is enthusiastic about change management, and actively seeks out innovative ways to discover new insights to facilitate business transformation. He is similarly passionate about building strong partnerships with his clients. These two goals keep him focused on providing actionable insights that have real-world impact for his clients.

Leonardo is a graduate of the Universidad Iberoamericana in business administration with two diploma degrees in marketing and top executive management.

Roger Sant

Roger Sant is head of global client solutions for Ipsos Loyalty. He leads a team that oversees Ipsos loyalty intellectual property—our offer—with the goal of continuously innovating, disseminating, and supporting.

Roger started his career as a nuclear scientist for the UK Ministry of Defence before deciding that management consultancy and then market research would be more of a challenge. Prior to joining Ipsos, Roger was on the European Board of Maritz research, responsible for research solutions and the European P&L (profit-and-loss) for financial services and telecommunications. He lived and worked in the United States for six years and has held leadership roles in a number of major research agencies.

Roger is considered a thought leader in customer experience measurement and management programs. He is a regular speaker at conferences and is the author of many articles, papers, and blogs. He has a master's degree in management science from the University of Warwick and a joint honours degree in mathematics and physics. In his spare time he has enjoyed county-level rugby, 50 free-fall parachute jumps, three bungee jumps, and one New York marathon.

Hans-Joachim Schuetze

Hans-Joachim Schuetze is associate manager for Ipsos Germany, where he leads Ipsos Loyalty's financial services team. He is passionate about bringing high-quality research results to life, enabling the entire organization to use up-to-date insights relevant to decision making. The core of his work for Ipsos is developing strategic and operational recommendations for his clients' senior management.

Prior to joining Ipsos, Hans-Joachim managed research projects across Europe for McKinsey & Company. Prior to this, he served as vice president in Bank of America's credit card customer insights group. He holds a diploma in psychology from the University of Mannheim, Germany, and an MBA from University of Maryland, College Park.

Mustapha Tabba

Mustapha Tabba currently holds the post of chief operating officer for Ipsos MENAP, part of the Ipsos Group. He also heads loyalty practice within the MENAP region. Mustapha graduated from the University of Maryland with a BS in marketing. He founded Tabba' & Associates Marketing Consultants in 1991, before partnering with the Ipsos Group in 1998. He has served as president of the International Advertising Association (IAA-Jordan Chapter), and was a founding member of the Young Entrepreneurs Association. He also served as a board member for the Young Arab Leaders Association. He currently serves as a board member for the Jordan Football Federation (FIFA Chapter) and is a member of the board of trustees for the Royal Health Awareness Society. Mustapha is also the author of the book, *Establish Your Own Venture: A Complete Guide on How to Start Your Own Business in Jordan*, which was published by YEA in 2000.

Simon Tye

Simon Tye is executive director at Ipsos Asia Pacific. He has worked for more than 15 years in the market research industry. He has broad experience across a number of industry sectors and customer groups, such as banking, finance, and premium/luxury (covering luxury brands, private banks, automotive, hospitality and airlines). Moreover, his breadth of knowledge and experience includes branding, advertising tracking, brand positioning, competitive analysis of brands and products, evaluating customer satisfaction with services and quality, consumer segmentation, distribution, channel development, and product testing research.

Simon is an expert in global luxury/premium brands and consumers. As such, he is a regular contributor to publications on consumer trends in luxury purchase behavior.

Simon is a graduate of Ohio Northern University.

James Vaughan

James Vaughan is an Ipsos research director with almost 15 years of experience in the field of customer and employee loyalty, currently based in Brazil. He is responsible for the management of several key accounts, as well as leading in the development of real-time, customer-centric research solutions in the region.

In his previous role as director of the Ipsos Loyalty Global Modeling Unit, he worked with diverse industry sectors and clients across the globe, designing and implementing modeling frameworks that underlie Ipsos products, including working extensively on the development of the driver model linked to the wallet allocation technique.

James is a graduate of the University of Manchester Institute of Science and Technology with a degree in information and technology management.

Farida Zaouai

Farida Zaouai is head of Ipsos Loyalty in the United Arab Emirates. In this role, she oversees all satisfaction- and loyalty-related research for the region.

Farida has 15 years of experience in market research, including satisfaction and loyalty, attitude and usage, choice modeling, and brand tracking. Her expertise centers on complex quantitative analytics. Much of her work has focused on the financial services sector, where she has extensive experience working with such firms as AXA, Société Générale Group, Barclays, Emirates NBD, and Abu Dhabi Commercial Bank.

Farida has a master's degree in marketing from Montpellier University (France) and in management from the Université Paris Dauphine.

Akmal Zoheir

Akmal Zoheir is head of research for Qatar and Bahrain at Ipsos. Prior to this, he was a research director at Ipsos in Egypt.

Akmal has almost 15 years of experience in the market research industry. During this time, he has gained broad-ranging experience across numerous industry sectors such as fast-moving consumer goods (FMCG), telecommunications, banking, automotives, and pharmaceutical industries. He is passionate about gleaning important insights from market research data, and using these insights to provide actionable recommendations for new product development, consumer segment identification, and alternate advertising techniques.

Akmal received his MBA in marketing and management from Murray State University in the United States.

Utmost Thanks

It is impossible to thank all of the people who provided support in the writing of this book. The first person we must thank, however, is our cocreator of the Wallet Allocation Rule, Professor Bruce Cooil of Vanderbilt University's Owen Graduate School of Management. You are first and foremost a cherished friend. You are also one of the most brilliant minds we will ever know.

Similarly, the contributions of Professor Sunil Gupta of the Harvard Business School are infused throughout this book. We have learned so much from our work together uncovering many of the problems connecting satisfaction (and Net Promoter Score) to business performance. Moreover, the ramifications of our findings, which appeared in the *MIT Sloan Management Review* and a Harvard Business School Case Note, represent cornerstones of this book.

Our work with Professors Bo Edvardsson, Phil Klaus, and Thorsten Gruber is immediately visible in Chapter 1 of this book. In fact, the book begins with chief executive officer (CEO) quotes and insights obtained through our research together. Our research regarding the loss of strategic influence of chief marketing officers (CMOs) (and marketing in general) within organizations galvanized us. As a result, it compelled us to infuse this book with practical tools that managers can use right now to address many of the most pressing problems for CMOs and CEOs.

Our work with Bruce Cooil, Ed Malthouse, Bart Lariviere, and Arne De Keyser is core to our validation of the Wallet Allocation Rule and plays a critical role in Chapter 2 of this book. Bruce, Ed, Bart, and Arne—all brilliant academic researchers—pushed us hard to test the limits of the Wallet Allocation Rule, and to understand why it works.

Our highest praise and thanks go out to our colleagues at Ipsos Loyalty and Fordham University. Your dedication, imagination, talent, and unwavering support for uncovering new and better ideas—even when they challenge long-held beliefs—provide us with a wellspring of inspiration.

We are especially grateful to Henri Wallard, Ralf Ganzenmueller, Alexandre Guérin, Liz Musch, and Matt McNerney who provided us with both financial resources and constant encouragement in our pursuit of a better way, without which we never would have discovered the Wallet Allocation Rule. We are similarly indebted to Pierre Le Manh and Jeff Cail for their invaluable support of the Wallet Allocation Rule and for the creation of this book.

We cannot thank Jason Verell enough for his unremitting help and positive attitude as we struggled to get this book off the ground; for over one year, Jason had a list of things that needed to happen to make this book a reality on his wall—and he made it happen.

There are no words to express the gratitude we have for John Carroll III, whose unwavering, vocal championing of this book and his relentless exploration of every avenue possible to see to it that we had what we needed transformed this book from a wish to a reality.

We were fortunate to have three tireless champions and wonderful friends in Roger Sant, Jean-Francois Damais, and John O'Neill to support us every step of the way.

We are extremely grateful to our wonderful literary agent, Michael Ebeling of Ebeling and Associates. You have been a friend to us for many years now. Thank you for sharing our vision, and for being such a wonderful person.

We are grateful to Matthew Holt of John Wiley & Sons for believing in and supporting *The Wallet Allocation Rule*. Without this commitment to publishing our ideas, *The Wallet Allocation Rule* would be little more than a message in a bottle.

This book benefited immensely from the work of Marina Koren, our editor, whose comments on style and substance helped transform our manuscript into something far more readable than we could have accomplished on our own. We have worked with many editors during development of our prior books. You are simply the best.

We are indebted to Titus Keiningham for his outstanding work in preparing the graphics used throughout this book.

Without question, there are many thought leaders who paved the way for our discovery of the Wallet Allocation Rule. In our opinion, the most important of these is Jan Hofmeyr, who with his colleagues discovered that the relationship between perceptual metrics (such as consumer satisfaction) and wallet share followed Zipf's law. Without this groundbreaking discovery, we may have never discovered the Wallet Allocation Rule.

Our deepest thanks go to our families, who provided encouragement and emotional support while suffering the many hours we were forced to spend researching and writing. To Hana Keiningham, Sage Keiningham, Max Keiningham, Anna Koren, Arleen Buoye, and Xavier Buoye, thank you for your love, patience, and understanding—we love you more than words can convey!

Finally, we would like to end by saying how blessed and thankful we feel to God for having given us the opportunity to write this book, and to meet and work with so many wonderful people along this incredible journey.

On behalf of Timothy Keiningham and Lerzan Aksoy we would like to add the following:

We would like to give our greatest thanks to our wonderful families for their unwavering support and having such a positive influence on so much of what makes us who we are today. We want to thank our parents, Lillie Keiningham, Thomas Lee Keiningham, Kathy Keiningham, Ihsan Aksoy, and Semra Aksoy, for their guidance, incredible resilience, and inspiration. We want to thank our children, Hana Keiningham, Sage Keiningham, and Max Keiningham, for making us want to work hard to make a better world for you to live in. Our sincere gratitude goes to our siblings and their beautiful families: Titus Keiningham, Katrin Keiningham, Alexander Keiningham, Christopher Keiningham, Pelin Kurtay, Miray Kurtay, Deren Kurtay, Levent Aksoy, Ebru Aksoy, Deniz Aksoy, Thomas Earl Keiningham, Donna Keiningham, Kristopher Keiningham, and Lee Ann Ward for always being there for us. A very special thanks to our closest friends Ahu Parlar Ozay and Sebnem Avsar for the emotional support, intellectual stimulation and laughter we always share—we cherish it deeply. Finally, it would also be remiss of us if we did not acknowledge the immense impact that the academic institutions we attended over the years have had on us personally and professionally. To Kentucky Wesleyan College, Vanderbilt University's Owen Graduate School of Management, Staffordshire University, Hacettepe University, George Mason University, and University of North Carolina–Chapel Hill: Thank you for instilling in us a desire for continuous learning and improvement, and for reinforcing the devotion necessary to achieve our dreams. Tim would like to end by thanking his wife and partner in everything that matters, Lerzan. I feel like country music singer (and my favorite songwriter) Phil Vassar wrote "Lucky As Me" based on my life with you. To paraphrase liberally: I've got an angel, so as long as you're standing by me, no one is as lucky as me.

On behalf of Luke Williams we would like to add the following:

I would like to thank, first and foremost, my loving wife, Anna. Her patience and support makes pursuing my dreams both possible and worthwhile. I would like to thank my family: George, Katherine, Scott, Monicka, Kavi, Shelley, Merilee, Patricia, Judy, and the rest of the clan. I would also like to thank my wife's family: Alexander, Lubov, and Marina. Many deep thanks also go to my many friends in the United States and abroad who suffer my absence when my passions (such as this book) take over. I would also like to pay special homage to the constant memories of George Williams and Matthew Gibney, two men who are dearly missed every day. Last, I would like to pay special tribute to those institutions that educated me and helped me to become the person I am today, each teaching me different and essential life lessons: the Delbarton School, Northfield Mount Hermon, St. Lawrence University, Rutgers University and the University of Durham. These are among the best schools in the United States and United Kingdom, and I am grateful for my experiences and opportunities at each.

On behalf of Alexander Buoye we would like to add the following:

Alex would like to extend his gratitude to his wife, Arleen, and son, Xavier, for giving him a reason to get up every morning; his parents, John and Lucy, for … well, for everything; his brothers, Brian and Jason; sister-in-law, Yvonne Sison; and Arleen's family: Rosie, Crispin, Jesus, and Russel Revilla, for their love and support; Sebastian Powell and J. Kennedy, for their lifelong friendship and counsel; former colleagues at Ipsos and Experian for showing him how to do the job; and last, members of the business and sociology faculty at the University of Notre Dame. Go Irish!

About the Authors

Timothy Keiningham, PhD

Tim Keiningham is global chief strategy officer at Ipsos Loyalty, the world's leading professional services firm dedicated exclusively to customer experience, satisfaction, and loyalty with in excess of 1,100 dedicated expert staff located in more than 80 countries.

A prolific writer, Tim has authored or edited nine books. He also works to expand the science and practice of marketing and management and has published numerous papers in leading management journals (e.g., *Harvard Business Review* and *MIT Sloan Management Review*) and leading academic journals (e.g., *Journal of Marketing, Marketing Science, Journal of the Academy of Marketing Science, Journal of Service Research,* and *Journal of Service Management*). Tim's research has received more than a dozen prestigious scientific awards, including the following:

- INFORMS Society for Marketing Science, top 20 most influential articles of the past 25 years
- Marketing Science Institute / H. Paul Root Award from the *Journal of Marketing* for the article judged to represent the most significant contribution to the advancement of the practice of marketing (twice)
- Citations of Excellence "Top 50" Award (top 50 management papers of approximately 20,000 papers reviewed that year) from Emerald Management Reviews
- Service Excellence Award (best paper) from the *Journal of Service Research*
- Outstanding Paper Award (best paper) from the journal *Managing Service Quality* (twice)

Tim received a BA from Kentucky Wesleyan College (USA), an MBA from Vanderbilt University (USA), and a PhD from Staffordshire University (UK).

Lerzan Aksoy, PhD

Lerzan Aksoy is professor of marketing at Fordham University Schools of Business in New York City. She is widely regarded as one of the leading experts in the measurement and management of customer satisfaction and loyalty. She was recognized as the top young scientist of 2007 in Turkey by the Junior Chamber International, winning the TOYP Award for Scientific Leadership. Five years later, she received one of the most prestigious business and management awards in Turkey: the 2012 Management Honor Award (Yönetim Onur Ödülü), a lifetime achievement award for research contributions that affect management across international boundaries. Professor Aksoy also has received the Koç University Werner Von Siemens Award and the Fordham University Magis Award for research, teaching, and social contribution.

Lerzan has written or edited five books. Her articles have been accepted for publication in top-tier journals in marketing (e.g., the *Journal of Marketing, Marketing Science, Journal of the Academy of Marketing Science,* and *Journal of Interactive Marketing*), strategy (including *Harvard Business Review* and *MIT Sloan Management Review*), and service management (e.g., the *Journal of Service Research, Journal of Service Management,* and *Managing Service Quality*). Her research has received numerous prestigious scientific awards, including the following:

- Marketing Science Institute / H. Paul Root Award from the *Journal of Marketing* for the article judged to represent the most significant contribution to the advancement of the practice of marketing
- Citations of Excellence "Top 50" Award (top 50 management papers of approximately 20,000 papers reviewed that year) from Emerald Management Reviews
- Outstanding Paper Award (best paper) from the *Journal of Service Management*

- Outstanding Paper Award (best paper) from the journal *Managing Service Quality* (twice)
- Next Gen Disruptive Innovation Award in Market Research

Lerzan earned a BS from Hacettepe University in Ankara, Turkey, and was awarded the Fulbright Scholarship to pursue her MBA degree at George Mason University in Fairfax, Virginia. She earned a PhD in marketing from the University of North Carolina at Chapel Hill's Kenan Flagler Business School.

Luke Williams

Luke Williams is vice president at Ipsos Loyalty, where he leads the day-to-day activity of large-scale research engagements for the firm. He specializes in research methods and design, analytics planning, and the eliciting of strategy from research results.

Luke is coauthor of the book *Why Loyalty Matters: The Groundbreaking Approach to Rediscovering Happiness, Meaning, and Lasting Fulfillment in Your Life and Work*. Luke has also authored numerous articles that have appeared in publications such as the *Wall Street Journal, Journal of Service Research, Journal of Business Research, Journal of Database Marketing & Customer Strategy Management, Quirks Marketing Research Review, Marketing Management, Training & Development,* and *The Wise Marketer*. Luke has also coauthored four book chapters in scholarly books and a Harvard Business School case study.

Luke was a core member of the research team that discovered and developed the Wallet Allocation Rule. The Wallet Allocation Rule has won the Next Gen Disruptive Innovation Award and was introduced in the *Harvard Business Review*.

Luke received a master's degree in social research methods from the University of Durham (UK) and a bachelor's degree in sociology from Rutgers University (USA).

Alexander Buoye, PhD

Alexander Buoye is assistant professor of marketing at Fordham University Schools of Business. Prior to joining the Fordham faculty, Alex was head of loyalty analytics and senior vice president at Ipsos Loyalty, where he spent seven years overseeing all advanced analytics for the U.S. loyalty practice.

Alex's research focuses on customer satisfaction and its relationship to loyalty and firm performance. His work has been published in *Harvard Business Review, MIT Sloan Management Review,* and the *Wall Street Journal,* as well as leading scientific journals such as the *Journal of Service Research, Journal of Service Management, Journal of Business Research,* and *Journal of Interactive Marketing.* For his research he has been awarded the Next Gen Disruptive Innovation Award in Market Research (for his role in the discovery and development of the Wallet Allocation Rule) and the Best Practitioner Award from the Frontiers in Service conference.

Alex received his PhD and MA in sociology and a bachelor of business administration degree in marketing from the University of Notre Dame.

Notes

Preface

1. Brown, John Seely. "Research That Reinvents the Corporation." *Harvard Business Review* 69, no. 1 (January/February 1991): 102–111. Quote on page 109.

2. Keiningham, Timothy L., Terry G. Vavra, Lerzan Aksoy, and Henri Wallard. *Loyalty Myths: Hyped Strategies That Will Put You Out of Business.* Hoboken, NJ: John Wiley & Sons, 2005.

3. Rust, Roland T., Anthony J. Zahorik, and Timothy L. Keiningham. *Return on Quality: Measuring the Financial Impact of Your Company's Quest for Quality.* Burr Ridge, IL: Irwin Professional Publishing, 1994.

4. Keiningham, Timothy L., and Terry G. Vavra. *The Customer Delight Principle: Exceeding Customers' Expectations for Bottom-line Success.* New York, NY: McGraw-Hill/American Marketing Association, 2001.

5. Keiningham, Timothy, Lerzan Aksoy, and Luke Williams. *Why Loyalty Matters.* Dallas, TX: BenBella Books, 2009.

6. Keiningham, Timothy L., Lerzan Aksoy, Alexander Buoye, and Bruce Cooil. "Customer Loyalty Isn't Enough. Grow Your Share of Wallet," *Harvard Business Review* 89 (2011, October): 29–31.

7. "Ipsos Allocated Its Share at Market Research Innovation Awards," Ipsos Press Release, November 9, 2011, accessed September 27, 2013, http://www.ipsos-na.com/news-polls/pressrelease.aspx?id=5402.

8. Examples include Aksoy, Lerzan. "Linking Satisfaction to Share of Deposits: An Application of the Wallet Allocation Rule." *International Journal of Bank Marketing* 32, no. 1 (2013): 28–42; and Keiningham, Timothy L., Bruce Cooil, Edward C. Malthouse, Alexander Buoye, Lerzan Aksoy, Arne De Keyser, and Bart Larivière. "Perceptions Are Relative: An Examination of the Relationship between

Relative Satisfaction Metrics and Share of Wallet." *Journal of Service Management*, 26, no. 1 (2015), forthcoming.

Chapter 1

1. Davidow, William H. *Marketing High Technology*. New York, NY: The Free Press, 1986, p. 7.

2. Klaus, Phil, Bo Edvardsson, Timothy L. Keiningham, and Thorsten Gruber. "Getting in with the 'In' Crowd: How to Put Marketing Back on the CEO's Agenda." *Journal of Service Management* 25, no. 2 (2014): 195–212.

3. Ibid.

4. Keiningham, Timothy L., Lerzan Aksoy, Phil Klaus, Bo Edvardsson, and Thorsten Gruber. "From Marketing Myopia to Marketing Dystopia." Fordham University Working Paper. New York, NY, 2014.

5. Kranik, Pete. "CMO Impact on Customer Experience." *A Joint Survey by The CMO Club and Neolane (June)*, 2013, www.neolane.com /usa/resources/CMO-Survey-Report/cmo-club-survey-results.

6. Klaus, Edvardsson, Keiningham, and Gruber, "Getting in with the 'In' Crowd: How to Put Marketing Back on the CEO's Agenda."

7. Ibid.

8. Sisodia, Rajendra S. "Marketing's Reputation with Consumers and Business Professionals." *Proceedings of Symposium Does Marketing Need Reform?* Bentley College, Boston, MA, August 2004, http://atc3.bentley.edu/mkseminar/reformsisodia/msh.htm.

9. Drucker, Peter F. *The Practice of Management*. New York: Harper & Brothers, 1954, pp. 37–38.

10. Allen, James, Frederick F. Reichheld, and Barney Hamilton. "Tuning In to the Voice of Your Customer." *Harvard Management Update* (2005, October 1), http://hbr.org/product/tuning-into-the-voice-of -your-customer/an/U0510C-PDF-ENG.

11. Temkin, Bruce. "The State of Customer Experience Management, 2014." Waban, MA: Temkin Group, 2014.

12. McGrath, Rita Gunther. "How the Growth Outliers Do It." *Harvard Business Review* 90 (January–February 2012): 110–116.

13. Olson, Matthew S., Derek van Bever, and Seth Verry. "When Growth Stalls." *Harvard Business Review* 86 (March 2008): 50–61.

14. Farris, Paul W., Neil T. Bendle, Phillip E. Pfeifer, and David J. Reibstein. *Marketing Metrics: 50+ Metrics Every Executive Should Master.* Upper Saddle River, NJ: Wharton School Publishing, 2006, p. 27.

15. Ibid., p. 26

16. Ibid., p. 32

17. Ibid., p. 32

18. Weissenberg, Adam, Ashley Katz, and Anupam Narula. "A Restoration in Hotel Loyalty: Developing a Blueprint for Reinventing Loyalty Programs." Deloitte Development LLC, 2013.

19. Coyles, Stephanie, and Timothy C. Gokey. "Customer Retention Is Not Enough." *The McKinsey Quarterly,* no. 2 (2002): 81–89.

20. Jones, Thomas O., and W. Earl Sasser, Jr. "Why Satisfied Customers Defect." *Harvard Business Review* 73 (November-December 1995): 88–99.

21. Aksoy, Lerzan. "How Do You Measure What You Can't Define? The Current State of Loyalty Measurement and Management." *Journal of Service Management* 24, no. 4 (2013): 356–381.

22. CEO Challenge 2014, Conference Board Research Report R-1537–14-RR.

23. Temkin, "The State of Customer Experience Management"

24. For example, see the Customer Experience Professionals Association, http://www.cxpa.org/.

25. MENG Marketing Trends Report 2009, Anderson Analytics LLC, accessed August 27, 2013, http://www.slideshare.net/hubbudunya /meng-marketing-trends-report-2009.

26. Aksoy, "How Do You Measure What You Can't Define?"

27. Bradford, Harry. "10 Companies with the Best Customer Experience." *The Huffington Post,* September 20, 2011, accessed on September 6, 2013, http://www.huffingtonpost.com/2011/09/20 /the-top-10-companies-with-most-admired-customer-experience_n _972027.html.

28. Reichheld, Frederick F. "The One Number You Need to Grow." *Harvard Business Review* 81, no. 12 (2003): 46–55.

29. Hayes, Bob E. "Customer Loyalty 2.0." *Quirks Marketing Research Review* 57 (October 2008): 54–58, http://www.quirks.com/articles /2008/20081004.asp.

30. Keiningham, Timothy L., Bruce Cooil, Tor Wallin Andreassen, and Lerzan Aksoy. "A Longitudinal Examination of Net Promoter and Firm Revenue Growth." *Journal of Marketing* 71, no. 3 (July 2007): 39–51; Morgan, Neil A., and Lopo Leottte do Rego. "The Value of Different Customer Satisfaction and Loyalty Metrics in Predicting Business Performance." *Marketing Science* 25, no. 5 (September/ October 2006): 426–439; and Van Doorn, Jenny, Peter S.H. Leeflang, and Marleen Tijs. "Satisfaction as a Predictor of Future Performance: A Replication." *International Journal of Research in Marketing* 30, no. 3 (2013): 314–318.

31. "What Is Net Promoter?" accessed September 16, 2006, http://www .netpromoter.com/netpromoter/index.php.

32. Reichheld, Frederick F. *The Ultimate Question*. Boston, MA: Harvard Business School Publishing, 2006, pp. 192–194.

33. Reichheld, Frederick F. "Net Promoters." Bain Audio Presentation (February 24, 2004), slide 4, accessed August 27, 2013, http://resultsbrief.bain.com/videos/0402/main.html.

34. Van Doorn, Leeflang, and Tijs, "Satisfaction as a Predictor," p. 314.

35. Fornell, Claes. "The Quality of Economic Output: Empirical Generalizations about Its Distribution and Relationship to Market Share." *Marketing Science* 14, no. 3 (supplement, 1995): G203–G211.

36. Yahoo! Finance India. "The 10 Largest Employers in the World." April 10, 2013, accessed August 27, 2013, http://in.finance.yahoo .com/photos/the-10-largest-employers-in-the-world-slideshow/.

37. "Credit Unions Set All-Time Record for Customer Satisfaction," ACSI Press Release, December 2012, accessed August 28, 2013, http://www.theacsi.org/media-resources/press-release-december -2011.

38. Schenk, Mike. "Commercial Banks and Credit Unions: Facts, Fallacies, and Recent Trends Year-End 2012." Credit Union National Association (CUNA) (2012), accessed August 28, 2013, http://www .cuna.org/research-and-strategy/downloads/combanks_cus.

39. Rego, Lopo L., Neil A. Morgan, and Claes Fornell. "Reexamining the Market Share–Customer Satisfaction Link." *Journal of Marketing 77*, no. 5 (2013): 1–20.

40. Bulik, Beth Snyder. "How Jiffy Lube Used Its Net Promoter Score to Goose Sales." *Ad Age,* July 14, 2013, accessed August 27, 2013, http://adage.com/article/dataworks/jiffy-lube-net-promoter-score-goose-sales/243046/.

41. Numerous scientific investigations point to a statistically significant relationship between customer satisfaction and customers' buying behaviors. Examples include Bolton, Ruth N. "A Dynamic Model of the Duration of the Customer's Relationship with a Continuous Service Provider: The Role of Satisfaction." *Marketing Science* 17, no. 1 (1998): 45–65; Cooil, Bruce, Timothy L. Keiningham, Lerzan Aksoy, and Michael Hsu. "A Longitudinal Analysis of Customer Satisfaction and Share of Wallet: Investigating the Moderating Effect of Customer Characteristics." *Journal of Marketing* 71, no. 1 (2007): 67–83; Keiningham, Timothy L., Bruce Cooil, Lerzan Aksoy, Tor Wallin Andreassen, and Jay Weiner. "The Value of Different Customer Satisfaction and Loyalty Metrics in Predicting Customer Retention, Recommendation and Share-of-Wallet." *Managing Service Quality* 17, no. 4 (2017): 361–384; and Mittal, Vikas, and Wagner A. Kamakura. "Satisfaction, Repurchase Intent, and Repurchase Behavior: Investigating the Moderating Effect of Customer Characteristics." *Journal of Marketing Research* 38 (February 2001): 131–142.

42. Keiningham, Timothy L., Sunil Gupta, Lerzan Aksoy, and Alexander Buoye. "The High Price of Customer Satisfaction." *MIT Sloan Management Review* 55, no. 3 (Spring 2014): 37–46.

43. Keiningham, Timothy L., Bruce Cooil, Edward C. Malthouse, Alexander Buoye, Lerzan Aksoy, Arne De Keyser, and Bart Larivière. "Perceptions Are Relative: An Examination of the Relationship between Relative Satisfaction Metrics and Share of Wallet." *Journal of Service Management*, 26, no. 1 (2015), forthcoming.

44. Aksoy, Lerzan. "Linking Satisfaction to Share of Deposits: An Application of the Wallet Allocation Rule." *International Journal of Bank Marketing* 32, no. 1 (2014): 28–42.

45. Bliese, Paul D. "Within-Group Agreement, Non-Independence, and Reliability: Implications for Data Aggregation and Analysis," in *Multilevel Theory, Research, and Methods in Organizations,* eds. Katherine J. Klein and Steve W. J. Kozlowski. San Francisco, CA: Jossey-Bass, 2000, pp. 349–381.

46. Clancy, Kevin J., Paul D. Berger, and Thomas L. Magliozzi. "The Ecological Fallacy: Some Fundamental Research Misconceptions Corrected." *Journal of Advertising Research* 43, no. 04 (2003): 370–380; and Robinson, William S. "Ecological Correlations and the Behavior of Individuals." *American Sociological Review* 15, no. 3 (1950): 351–357.

47. "7 Billion: Are You Typical," YouTube video by *National Geographic Magazine,* last updated March 2, 2011, accessed September 13, 2013, http://www.youtube.com/watch?v=4B2xOvKFFz4.

48. Gregory, Sean. "Walmart's Latest Move to Crush the Competition." *Time,* September 9, 2009, accessed September 16, 2014 http://content.time.com/time/business/article/0,8599,1920698,00.html.

49. Crosby, Jackie. "Walmart's New Look Is More Than Skin Deep." *Star-Tribute,* December 19, 2009, accessed September 16, 2013, http://www.statesman.com/news/ap/business/walmarts-new-look-is-more-than-skin-deep-1/nRYbY/.

50. D'Innocenzio, Anne. "Wal-Mart: A Year of Taking Stock to Regain Footing." *Associated Press,* June 2, 2011, accessed September 16, 2013, http://cnsnews.com/news/article/wal-mart-year-taking-stock-regain-footing.

51. Dawson, Keith. "Wal-Mart Lost Billions Listening to Customers." *The CMO Site,* April 25, 2011, accessed September 16, 2013, http://www.thecmosite.com/author.asp?section_id=1200&doc_id=205973.

52. Banks, Richard. "Walmart Business Planning Falters: US Sales Down." Yahoo.com, February 23, 2011, accessed September 16, 2013, http://voices.yahoo.com/walmart-business-planning-falters-us-sales-down-7915792.html.

53. Dawson, "Wal-Mart Lost Billions Listening to Customers."

Chapter 2

1. Krucoff, Carol. "The 6 O'Clock Scholar: Librarian of Congress Daniel Boorstin and His Love Affair With Books." *Washington Post* (January 29, 1984): K1.

2. Kaufman, Leslie, and Claudia H. Deutsch. "Montgomery Ward to Close Its Doors," *New York Times* 150, no. 51617 (December 29, 2000): C1.

3. Blaug, Mark. *Economic Theory in Retrospect*, 5th ed. Cambridge, UK: Cambridge University Press, 1996, p. 309. Original German in Gossen, Hermann Heinrich. *Die Entwicklung der Gesetze des menschlichen Verkehrs und der daraus fließenden Regeln für menschliches Handeln* (1854).

4. For example, Cooil, Bruce, Timothy L. Keiningham, Lerzan Aksoy, and Michael Hsu. "A Longitudinal Analysis of Customer Satisfaction and Share of Wallet: Investigating the Moderating Effect of Customer Characteristics." *Journal of Marketing* 71, no. 1 (2007): 67–83; Keiningham, Timothy L., Tiffany Perkins-Munn, and Heather Evans. "The Impact of Customer Satisfaction on Share of Wallet in a Business-to-Business Environment." *Journal of Service Research* 6, no. 1 (August 2003): 37–50; and Van Doorn, Jenny, and Peter C. Verhoef. "Critical Incidents and the Impact of Satisfaction on Customer Share." *Journal of Marketing* 72, no. 4 (2008): 123–142.

5. Reichheld, Frederick F. *The Ultimate Question*. Boston, MA: Harvard Business School Publishing, 2006, p. 41.

6. Keiningham, Timothy L., Bruce Cooil, Tor Wallin Andreassen, and Lerzan Aksoy. "A Longitudinal Examination of Net Promoter and Firm Revenue Growth." *Journal of Marketing* 71, no. 3 (July 2007): 39–51; Morgan, Neil A., and Lopo Leottte do Rego. "The Value of Different Customer Satisfaction and Loyalty Metrics in Predicting Business Performance." *Marketing Science* 25, no. 5 (September/October 2006): 426–439; and Van Doorn, Jenny, Peter S.H. Leeflang, and Marleen Tijs. "Satisfaction as a Predictor of Future Performance: A Replication." *International Journal of Research in Marketing* 30, no. 3 (2013): 314–318.

7. Kohli, Rajeev, and Raaj Sah. "Some Empirical Regularities in Market Shares." *Management Science* 52, no. 11 (November 2006): 1792–1798.

8. Timothy L. Keiningham, Bruce Cooil, Edward C. Malthouse, Alexander Buoye, Lerzan Aksoy, Arne De Keyser, and Bart Larivière. "Perceptions Are Relative: An Examination of the Relationship between Relative Satisfaction Metrics and Share of Wallet." *Journal of Service Management*, 26, no. 1 (2015), forthcoming.

9. Keiningham, Timothy L., Lerzan Aksoy, Alexander Buoye, and Bruce Cooil. "Customer Loyalty Isn't Enough. Grow Your Share of Wallet." *Harvard Business Review* 89 (October 2011): 29–31.

10. "Ipsos Allocated Its Share at Market Research Innovation Awards," Ipsos Press Release, November 9, 2011, accessed September 27, 2013, http://www.ipsos-na.com/news-polls/pressrelease.aspx?id=5402.

11. Aksoy, Lerzan. "Linking Member Satisfaction to Share of Deposits: Applying the Wallet Allocation Rule in Credit Unions." Publication Number 290 (2/13). Madison, WI: Filene Research Institute, 2013, accessed September 27, 2013, http://filene.org/assets/pdf -reports/290_Share_Deposits.pdf.

12. Aksoy, Lerzan. "Linking Satisfaction to Share of Deposits: An Application of the Wallet Allocation Rule." *International Journal of Bank Marketing* 32, no. 1 (2013) 28–42.

13. It is important to note that the discrete distributions examined perform remarkably well. Nine of the eleven discrete distributions — including the Wallet Allocation Rule — have root mean squared error (RMSE) values that are within 1.5 percent of the best fit. Nearly all of the discrete distributions perform at the same level when predicting change in share of wallet. The Wallet Allocation Rule, however, was by far the simplest of the models examined.

14. Timothy L. Keiningham, Bruce Cooil, Edward C. Malthouse, Alexander Buoye, Lerzan Aksoy, Arne De Keyser, and Bart Larivière, "Perceptions Are Relative."

15. Louw, Alice, and Jan Hofmeyr. "Reality Check in the Digital Age: The Relationship between What We Ask and What People Actually Do," in *3D Digital Dimensions 2012* (ESOMAR Publication Series Volume S355: ISBN 920831–0261–4), ed. Deborah S. Fellows. Amsterdam, The Netherlands: ESOMAR, 2012.

16. There is no statistically meaningful difference in the correlations of the three models investigated by Louw and Hofmeyr (2012). To quote Louw and Hofmeyr, "The three wallet estimation procedures perform similarly" (p. 14). The maximum difference between correlations for any of the models investigated was 0.04, with the average difference across all industries examined being 0.02. Moreover, the improved performance of the Power of Mind measure investigated rests on its using two questions to gauge rank, as opposed to using one for the other models investigated. Had the same questions been used to test all models, we are confident that these small differences between the Wallet Allocation Rule, Attitudinal Equity, and Power of the Mind models tested would have been virtually eliminated.

17. Zipf, George K. *The Psycho-Biology of Language: An Introduction to Dynamic Philology*. Boston, MA: Houghton Mifflin, 1935.

18. Little, John D. "Comments on 'Models and Managers: The Concept of a Decision Calculus': Managerial Models for Practice." *Management Science* 50, no. 12 (supplement December 2004): 1855.

19. Keiningham, Timothy L., Lerzan Aksoy, Alexander Buoye, and Bruce Cooil, "Customer Loyalty Isn't Enough," p. 30.

Chapter 3

1. Koestler, Arthur. *The Act of Creation*. London: Hutchinson & Co. (published by London: Arkana in 1989), 1964, p. 98.

2. Richardson, Kari, and Matt Golosinski. "The Business of Brand," Kellogg School of Management: News and Events, April 1, 2004, accessed August 19, 2014, http://www.kellogg.northwestern.edu /news_articles/2004/brandbusiness.aspx.

3. Edwards, Jim. "The 10 Biggest Advertisers In America, Ranked By Dollars Spent Annually." *Business Insider,* July 8, 2013, accessed August 19, 2014, http://www.businessinsider.com/the-10-biggest -advertisers-in-america-ranked-by-dollars-spent-annually-2013–7.

4. Keiningham, Timothy L., Bruce Cooil, Edward C. Malthouse, Alexander Buoye, Lerzan Aksoy, Arne De Keyser, and Bart Larivière. "Perceptions Are Relative: An Examination of the Relationship between Relative Satisfaction Metrics and Share of Wallet." *Journal of Service Management*, 26, no. 1 (2015), forthcoming.

5. Ellis, Blake. "Credit Unions Hit a Record Number of Members." CNNMoney, March 1, 2012, accessed August 26, 2014, http://money.cnn.com/2012/02/29/pf/credit_unions_members/.

6. "Credit Unions Set All-Time Record for Customer Satisfaction," ACSI Press Release, December 2012, accessed August 28, 2013, http ://www.theacsi.org/media-resources/press-release-december-2011.

7. Credit Union Strategy & Performance (CUSP) Online, 3rd Quarter 2010, p. 22, http://digital.turn-page.com/issue/24868/33; and Mike Werstuik. "Benchmarking Deposit Share—A Look at the Trends and Leaders," CreditUnions.com, March 12, 2007, http://www .creditunions.com/benchmarking-deposit-share-a-look-at-the-trends -and-leaders/.

8. The results of this investigation were published in Aksoy, Lerzan. "Linking Member Satisfaction to Share of Deposits: Applying the Wallet Allocation Rule in Credit Unions." Publication Number 290 (2/13). Madison, WI: Filene Research Institute, 2013, accessed September 27, 2013, http://filene.org/assets/pdf-reports/290_Share _Deposits.pdf; and Aksoy, Lerzan. "Linking Satisfaction to Share of Deposits: An Application of the Wallet Allocation Rule." *International Journal of Bank Marketing* 32, no. 1 (2013): 28–42.

9. Payments Council (2013), "Current Account Switch Guarantee," Available at: http://www.paymentscouncil.org.uk/switch_service /current_account_switch_guarantee/

10. "Old-fashioned but in favour; Germany's banking system." *The Economist* (November 10, 2012): 77, http://www.economist.com /news/finance-and-economics/21566013-defending-three-pillars -old-fashioned-favour.

Chapter 4

1. *I Love Lucy*, "The Million-Dollar Idea," Season 3, Episode 13, first aired January 11, 1954.

2. Tanner, Jeff, and Mary Anne Raymond. *Principles of Marketing* (Chapter 14). Washington, DC: Flat World Knowledge, 2010.

3. Reichheld, Frederick F. *The Ultimate Question*. Boston, MA: Harvard Business School Publishing, 2006, p. 45.

4. Ibid., p. 132.

5. Ibid., p. 149.

6. Ibid., p. 87.

7. "How Is Net Promoter Score^{SM} related to growth?" Net Promoter System^{SM}, accessed October 9, 2013, http://www.netpromotersystem .com/about/how-is-nps-related-to-growth.aspx.

8. Reichheld, *The Ultimate Question,* p. 45.

9. Ibid., p. 132.

10. Ibid., p. 46.

11. Ibid., p. 144.

12. Colgate, Mark, and Rachel Hedge. "An Investigation into the Switching Process in Retail Banking Services." *International Journal of Bank Marketing* 19, no. 4 (2001): 201–212.

13. Finkelstein, Brad. "HomeBanc Resurrected." *National Mortgage News* 32, no. 28 (April 14, 2008): 6.

14. Rust, Roland T., Anthony J. Zahorik, and Timothy L. Keiningham. *Return on Quality.* Chicago, IL: Probus Publishing, 1994, pp. 1–4.

15. Ivey, Mark, and John Carey. "The Ecstasy and the Agony." *Business Week* (October 21, 1991): 40.

16. Sixel, L.M. "Quality-Award Winner Files for Chapter 11." *The Houston Chronicle* (January 30, 1992): Business Section, p. 1.

17. Sixel, L.M. "Baldrige Winner Wallace Co. Sold to Louisiana Firm." *The Houston Chronicle* (August 5, 1992): Business Section, p. 2.

18. For example, Reichheld, Frederick F., and W. Earl Sasser, Jr. "Zero Defections: Quality Comes to Services," *Harvard Business Review* 68, no. 5 (1990): 105–111.

19. For example, Reichheld, *The Ultimate Question,* p. 51.

20. Keiningham, Timothy L., Terry G. Vavra, Lerzan Aksoy, and Henri Wallard. Loyalty Myths: Hyped Strategies That Will Put You Out of Business. Hoboken, NJ: John Wiley & Sons, 2005.

21. Reichheld, Frederick F., and W. Earl Sasser, Jr. "Zero Defections," p. 106.

22. Reinartz, Werner, and V. Kumar. "On the Profitability of Long-Life Customers in a Noncontractual Setting: An Empirical Investigation

and Implications for Marketing." *Journal of Marketing* 64, no. 4 (2000): 17–35; and Reinartz, Werner, and V. Kumar. "The Mismanagement of Customer Loyalty." *Harvard Business Review* 80, no. 7 (2007): 86–94.

23. Finnie, William, and Robert M. Randall. "Loyalty as a Philosophy and Strategy: An Interview with Frederick F. Reichheld." *Strategy & Leadership* 30, no. 2 (2002): 25–31.

24. Reinartz, W., and V. Kumar, "On the Profitability of Long-Life Customers"; and Reinartz, W., and V. Kumar, "The Mismanagement of Customer Loyalty."

25. El Boghdady, Dina. "Giving Discounts Where It Counts; More Retailers Using Coupons to Lure Biggest Spenders." *The Washington Post* (December 19, 2003).

26. Aksoy, Lerzan. "How Do You Measure What You Can't Define? The Current State of Loyalty Measurement and Management." *Journal of Service Management* 24, no. 4 (2013): 356–381.

27. Aksoy, Lerzan, Alexander Buoye, Bruce Cooil, Timothy L. Keiningham, DeDe Paul, and Chris Volinsky. "Can We Talk? The Impact of Willingness to Recommend on a New-to-Market Service Brand Extension within a Social Network." *Journal of Service Research* 14, no. 3 (August 2011): 355–371.

28. Anderson, E. W. "Customer Satisfaction and Word-of-Mouth." *Journal of Service Research* 1, no. 1 (1998): 1–14; and Oliver, Richard L. *Satisfaction: A Behavioral Perspective on the Consumer,* 2nd ed. Armonk, NY: M.E. Sharpe, 2010.

29. East, Robert, Kathy Hammond, and Malcolm Wright. "The Relative Incidence of Positive and Negative Word of Mouth: A Multi-Category Study." *International Journal of Research in Marketing* 24, no. 2 (2007): 175–184.

30. Godes, David, and Dina Mayzlin. "Firm-Created Word-of-Mouth Communication: A Field-Based Quasi-Experiment." Harvard Business School Marketing Research Paper No. 04–03, 2004.

31. Godes, David, and Dina Mayzlin. "Using Online Conversations to Study Word-of-Mouth Communication." *Marketing Science* 23, no. 4 (Fall 2004): 545–560; and Yu, Larry. "How Companies Turn Buzz

into Sales." *MIT Sloan Management Review* 46, no. 2 (Winter 2005): 5–6.

32. Kumar, V., J. Andrew Petersen, and Robert P. Leone. "How Valuable Is Word of Mouth?" *Harvard Business Review* 85, no. 10 (October 2007): 140.

33. Reichheld, Frederick F., and W. Earl Sasser, Jr., "Zero Defections."

34. Carroll, Peter. "The Fallacy of Customer Retention." *Journal of Retail Banking* 13, no. 4 (Winter 1991–1992): 15–20; East, Robert, Kathy Hammond, and Philip Gendall. "Fact and Fallacy in Retention Marketing." *Journal of Marketing Management* 22, no. 1–2 (2006): 5–23; and Keiningham, Timothy L., Terry G. Vavra, Lerzan Aksoy, and Henri Wallard. *Loyalty Myths: Hyped Strategies That Will Put You Out of Business.* Hoboken, NJ: John Wiley & Sons, 2005, pp. 50–52.

35. Gupta, Sunil, Donald Lehmann, and Jennifer Ames Stuart. "Valuing Customers." *Journal of Marketing Research* 41, no. 1 (2004): 7–18.

36. Coyles, Stephanie, and Timothy C. Gokey. "Customer Retention Is Not Enough." *The McKinsey Quarterly* 2, no. 2 (2002): 81–89.

37. Keiningham, Timothy L., Lerzan Aksoy, Yuliya A. Komarova, and Mohammad G. Nejad. "The Chain of Effects from Customer Satisfaction to Customer Profitability: Repairing Broken Connections," in *Handbook of Research on Customer Equity,* eds. V. Kumar and Denish Shah. Edward Elgar Publishing House, 2015, pp. 265–282.

38. Keiningham, Timothy L., Terry G. Vavra, Lerzan Aksoy, and Henri Wallard, *Loyalty Myths,* pp. 43–44.

39. Kaplan, Robert S., and V.G. Narayanan. "Customer Profitability Measurement and Management," White Paper, May 2001, Houston, TX: Acorn Systems, Inc., http://www.acornsys.com/value/whitepapers/WP-CustomerProfitabilityMM.html.

40. Tanner, Jeff, and Mary Anne Raymond. "Customer Satisfaction," in *Principles of Marketing* (Chapter 14.3). Washington, DC: Flat World Knowledge, 2010.

41. *Field of Dreams* quote, IMDb, accessed on November 11, 2013, http://www.imdb.com/title/tt0097351/quotes.

42. "Short-termism," Oxford Dictionaries, accessed October 13, 2013, http://oxforddictionaries.com/us/definition/american_english /short—termism.

43. Jagannathan, Ravi, Mudit Kapoor, and Ernst Schaumburg. "What Really Spurred the Great Recession?" *Kellogg Insight,* July 1, 2013, accessed November 11, 2013,http://insight.kellogg.northwestern .edu/article/what_really_spurred_the_great_recession/.

44. Adamy, Janet. "U.S. Ties Hospital Payments to Making Patients Happy." *Wall Street Journal* (October 14, 2012): A1.

45. Ibid.

46. Goldman, Dana P., and John A. Romley. "Hospitals as Hotels: The Role of Patient Amenities in Hospital Demand," NBER Working Paper 14619, April 19, 2010, accessed November 11, 2013, http:// www-bcf.usc.edu/~romley/Hospitals_As_Hotels_current.pdf.

47. James, John T. "A New, Evidence-based Estimate of Patient Harms Associated with Hospital Care." *Journal of Patient Safety* 9, no. 3 (September 2013): 122–128.

48. Rosenberg, Tina. "To Make Hospitals Less Deadly, a Dose of Data." *New York Times,* December 4, 2013, accessed December 5, 2013, http://opinionator.blogs.nytimes.com/2013/12/04/to-make -hospitals-less-deadly-a-dose-of-data/?_r=0.

49. Rosenthal, Elisabeth. "Is This a Hospital or a Hotel?" *New York Times* (September 22, 2013): SR12.

50. Fenton, Joshua J., Anthony F. Jerant, Klea D. Bertakis, and Peter Franks. "The Cost of Satisfaction: A National Study of Patient Satisfaction, Health Care Utilization, Expenditures, and Mortality." *Archives of Internal Medicine* 172, no. 5 (March 12, 2012): 405–411.

51. Brown, Theresa. "Hospitals Aren't Hotels." *New York Times* (March 15, 2012): A35.

52. Gupta, Sunil, Timothy Keiningham, Ray Weaver, and Luke Williams. "Are Daily Deals Good for Merchants?" Harvard Business School Industry and Background Note 513–059, December 2012, http://cb.hbsp.harvard.edu/cb/web/product_detail.seam?E= 4726234&R=513059-PDF-ENG&conversationId=1311046.

53. Stern, Philip, and Kathy Hammond. "The Relationship between Customer Loyalty and Purchase Incidence." *Marketing Letters* 15, no. 1 (2004): 5–19.

54. One of the most popular methods used to focus on customer level profitability is through the use of customer lifetime value (CLV) analysis. For readers interested in learning more about CLV, we recommend: Gupta, Sunil, and Donald R. Lehmann. *Managing Customers as Investments.* Upper Saddle River, NJ: Pearson Education/Wharton School Publishing, 2005; Kumar, V. *Managing Customers for Profit.* Upper Saddle River, NJ: Pearson Education/Prentice Hall, 2008; and Malthouse, Edward. *Segmentation and Lifetime Value Models Using SAS.* Cary, NC: The SAS Institute, 2013.

55. Keiningham, Timothy L., Terry G. Vavra, Lerzan Aksoy, and Henri Wallard, *Loyalty Myths,* pp. 38–40.

56. Drucker, Peter F. *The Practice of Management.* New York: Harper & Brothers, 1954, p. 46.

Chapter 5

1. Hastie, Trevor, Robert Tibshirani, and Jerome Friedman. *The Elements of Statistical Learning,* 2nd ed. New York: Springer, 2009, p. vii.

2. Kliff, Sarah. "Surprise! We Don't Know If Half Our Medical Treatments Work." *The Washington Post,* WONKBLOG, January 24, 2013, accessed November 15, 2013, http://www.washington post.com/blogs/wonkblog/wp/2013/01/24/surprise-we-dont-know-if-half-our-medical-treatments-work/.

3. "What Conclusions Has *Clinical Evidence* Drawn About What Works, What Doesn't Based on Randomised Controlled Trial Evidence?" *Clinical Evidence,* 2012, accessed November 15, 2013, http://clinicalevidence.bmj.com/x/set/static/cms/efficacy-categorisa tions.html.

4. For an excellent review, we direct the reader to David H. Newman, *Hippocrates' Shadow.* New York, NY: Scribner/Simon & Schuster, 2008.

5. Pfeffer, Jeffrey, and Robert I. Sutton. "Evidence-Based Management." *Harvard Business Review* 84, no. 1 (January 2006): 62–74.

6. Newman, David H. "Believing in Treatments That Don't Work." *New York Times, Wellness Blog,* April 2, 2009, accessed November 16, 2013, http://well.blogs.nytimes.com/2009/04/02/the-ideology-of-health-care/?_r=0.

7. Pfeffer and Sutton, "Evidence-Based Management," p. 64.

8. Ibid., p. 67.

9. Rosenzweig, Phil. *The Halo Effect … and the Eight Other Business Delusions That Deceive Managers.* New York, NY: The Free Press, 2007, p. 69.

10. For example, although the *Harvard Business Review* (*HBR*) is highly regarded by both managers and academics, it is not a peer-reviewed journal. Without question, *HBR* is an outstanding source of new management ideas. Claims based on data in the journal, however, still need to be subjected to rigorous review before being presumed to be generalizable. In the case of the Wallet Allocation Rule, it both was introduced to managers in the *Harvard Business Review* and has undergone several peer-reviewed examinations that were published in leading scientific journals.

11. Du, Rex Yuxing, Wagner A. Kamakura, and Carl F. Mela. "Size and Share of Customer Wallet." *Journal of Marketing* 71, no. 2 (April 2007): 94–113.

12. Keiningham, Timothy L., Sunil Gupta, Lerzan Aksoy, and Alexander Buoye. "The High Price of Customer Satisfaction." *MIT Sloan Management Review* 55, no. 3 (Spring 2014): 37–46.

13. A detailed review of key driver methodologies is beyond the scope of this book. For readers interested in a thorough review, we direct them to the following: Buoye, Alexander, Timothy L. Keiningham, Luke Williams, and Lerzan Aksoy. "Understanding What It Takes to Be Number 1," in *Customer Experience Management: Enhancing Experience and Value Through Service Management,* ed. Jay Kandampully. Dubuque, IA: Kendall Hunt Publishing, 2014, pp. 327–345.

14. Buoye, Alexander. "Linking Satisfaction to Share of Grocery Spending: An International Application of the Wallet Allocation Rule (WAR)," Fordham University Working Paper, 2014.

15. Hawkins, Rosie. "The Commitment Economy," TNS White Paper, 2012, accessed November 25, 2013, http://www.tnsglobal.com/sites/default/files/whitepaper/TNS_Commitment_Economy_Cant_Always_Get_What_You_Want_0.pdf.

16. Hawkins, "The Commitment Economy."

17. Daniel, Colin. *The Big Fat South African Joke Book.* Cape Town, South Africa: Zebra Press/Struik Publishers, 2004, p. 112.

Chapter 6

1. "National Affairs: Foreign Policy: Ike," *Time Magazine,* October 06, 1952, accessed December 17, 2013, http://content.time.com/time/magazine/article/0,9171,890303,00.html.

2. Wilson, Woodrow. Address at the Salesmanship Congress, Detroit, Michigan (July 19, 1916), as reported in *President Wilson's State Papers and Addresses (1918),* ed. Albert Shaw. New York, NY: George H. Doran, 1916, p. 286.

3. Laërtius, Diogenes. *Lives and Opinions of Eminent Philosophers* (originally believed to be written in the third century AD).

4. Rooney, Jennifer. "CMO Tenure Reaches 45 Months," *Forbes,* April 25, 2013, accessed April 29, 2013 http://www.forbes.com/sites/jenniferrooney/2013/04/25/cmo-tenure-now-averages-45-months/.

5. "The Conference Board CEO Succession Practices 2013 Edition," Conference Board Research Report TCB_R-1520–13-RR (April 2013), New York, NY: The Conference Board.

6. "The Conference Board CEO Challenge 2013," Conference Board Research Report R-1511–13-ES (October 2013), New York, NY: The Conference Board.

7. For example, Bursztajn, Harold J., and Richard Sobel. "Accountability without Health Care Data Banks," *Health Affairs* 17, no. 6 (1998): 252–253; Frase-Blunt, Martha. "Stalking the Killer in the Corridor—Hospitals Strive to Reduce Infection as Antibiotic Resistance Grows." *Hospital Topics* 77, no. 1 (1999): 4–8; and Magee, Maureen. "Students Given Role in Census of Marine Life." *U-T San Diego,* March 30, 2010, http://www.utsandiego.com/news/2010/mar/30/a-massive-science-project, accessed July 16, 2014.

8. Figures from Larry P. English, *Improving Data Warehouse and Business Information Quality: Methods for Reducing Costs and Increasing Profits*. New York: John Wiley & Sons, 1999; and Loshin, David. *Enterprise Knowledge Management: The Data Quality Approach*. San Francisco, CA: Morgan Kaufmann, 2001.

9. Tibbets, Hollis. "$3 Trillion Problem: Three Best Practices for Today's Dirty Data Pandemic." *SOA World Magazine*, September 10, 2011, http://soa.sys-con.com/node/1975126, accessed April 29, 2013.

10. The total sample size needed is almost always substantially smaller than the maximum possible because many customers will use multiple brands. Nonetheless, the sample size required to conduct a Wallet Allocation Rule analysis for your brand is typically much larger for a market representative sample than a customer-only sample.

11. For readers interested in a thorough review of methods of listening to customers and the design of customer satisfaction questionnaires, we direct them to the following: Rust, Roland T., Anthony J. Zahorik, and Timothy L. Keiningham. "Methods of Listening to the Customer" (Chapter 6), in *Service Marketing*. New York, NY: HarperCollins, 1996, pp. 155–178; and Rust, Roland T., Anthony J. Zahorik, and Timothy L. Keiningham. "Designing Customer Satisfaction Surveys" (Chapter 10), in *Service Marketing*. New York, NY: HarperCollins, 1996, pp. 240–256.

12. Favaro, Ken, David Meer, and Samrat Sharma. "Creating an Organic Growth Machine." *Harvard Business Review* 90, no. 5 (May 2012): 98.

13. *Knowledge@Wharton*, "Three Reasons Why Good Strategies Fail: Execution, Execution ..." *Knowledge@Wharton*, August 10, 2005, http://knowledge.wharton.upenn.edu/article/three-reasons-why-good-strategies-fail-execution-execution/, accessed April 29, 2013.

14. "Ipsos Allocated Its Share at Market Research Innovation Awards," Ipsos Press Release, November 9, 2011, accessed September 27, 2013, http://www.ipsos-na.com/news-polls/pressrelease.aspx?id=5402.

15. Drucker, Peter. *Management: Tasks, Responsibilities, Practices*. New York: Harper & Row Publishers, 1973, pp. 64–65.

What's Next

1. Huxley, Thomas Henry. (1877), "XVI: Technical Education" *Science & Education (Essays)*, 1877, accessed August 24, 2014, http://www.gutenberg.org/files/7150/7150–8.txt.

Appendix A

1. Quoted in Kennedy, Debbe, and Sally K. Green. *Putting Our Differences to Work*. San Francisco, CA: Berrett-Koehler Publishers, 2008, p. 43.

Appendix B

1. Sagan, Carl. *The Demon-Haunted World: Science as a Candle in the Dark*. New York, NY: Random House, 1996, p. 323.

2. The 40 percent and 1.4 brands used values are consistent with an estimated Dirichlet model S-parameter value of 0.8, which has been used in the academic literature to delineate repertoire and subscription markets. For more information, see Sharp, Byron, Malcolm Wright, and Gerald Goodhardt. "Purchase Loyalty Is Polarised into Either Repertoire or Subscription Patterns." *Australasian Marketing Journal* 10, no. 3 (2002): 7–20.

3. Discrete choice is a statistical technique for modeling the trade-offs that consumers make between the features and price of a product/service. For more information, see Train, Kenneth E. *Discrete Choice Methods with Simulation*. New York, NY: Cambridge University Press, 2009.

4. Keiningham, Timothy L., Lerzan Aksoy, Edward C. Malthouse, Alexander Buoye, and Bart Larivière. "The Cumulative Effect of Satisfaction with Discrete Transactions on Share of Wallet." *Journal of Service Management* 25, no. 3 (2014): 310–333.

5. Churchill, Gilbert A. Jr., and J. Paul Peter. "Research Design Effects on the Reliability of Rating Scales: A Meta-analysis." *Journal of Marketing*

Research 21, no. 4 (November 1984): 360–375; Friedman, Hershey H., and Linda Weiser Friedman. "On the Danger of Using Too Few Points in a Rating Scale: A Test of Validity." *Journal of Data Collection* 26, no. 2 (Fall 1984): 60–63; Martin, Warren S. "The Effects of Scaling on the Correlation Coefficient: A Test of Validity." *Journal of Marketing Research* 10, no. 3 (August 1973): 316–318; and Martin, Warren S. "Effects of Scaling on the Correlation Coefficient: Additional Considerations." *Journal of Marketing Research* 15, no. 2 (May 1978): 304–308.

6. Shares for truncated lists of brands can be rebased to the totals for the brands included in the questionnaire and the relative rankings should still produce accurate predictions of the relative shares.

7. Bliese, Paul D. "Within-Group Agreement, Non-independence, and Reliability: Implications for Data Aggregation and Analysis," in *Multilevel Theory, Research, and Methods in Organizations,* eds. Katherine J. Klein and Steve W. J. Kozlowski. San Francisco, CA: Jossey-Bass, 2000, pp. 349–381.

8. Buoye, Alexander, Yuliya Komarova, Sertan Kabadyi, Mohammad G. Nejad, Timothy L. Keiningham, Lerzan Aksoy, and Jason Allsopp. "Is Share of Wallet Really All about Market Share? Exploring the Relationship between Customer Satisfaction and the Double Jeopardy Rule," Fordham University Working Paper, 2014.

Acknowledgments

1. Lennon, John, and Paul McCartney, "With a Little Help from My Friends" (1967), which first appeared on the *Sgt. Pepper's Lonely Hearts Club Band* album by The Beatles. The song was first recorded on March 29, 1967; the Sgt. Pepper's album was released on June 1, 1967.

Index

Page references followed by *fig* indicate an illustrated figure; followed by *t* indicate a table.